SOUTHWESTERN MEN
and
THEIR MESSAGES

SOUTHWESTERN MEN

and

THEIR MESSAGES

Edited by

J. M. PRICE

Director, School of Religious Education

Southwestern Baptist Theological Seminary

Kansas City, Kansas

Central Seminary Press

1948

23,867

Printed by
Central Seminary Press
Kansas City, Kansas
U.S.A.

To Those

Whom These

Have Taught

CONTENTS

CONTENTS CONTINUED

FOREWORD

Southwestern Baptist Theological Seminary commemorates its fortieth anniversary this year, thus rounding out four decades of service. During these years the institution has had some of the greatest leaders in the South and they have made invaluable contributions.

It seems fitting, therefore, to bring out at this time a volume giving brief but comprehensive biographies of the lives of early leaders together with an outstanding sermon, address, or article from each. It is felt that former students and friends everywhere will be interested in having these materials for permanent records.

In the nature of the case it was impossible to include in one volume all of those who have contributed to the life of the institution. Therefore, there have been chosen twelve leaders of the early days who were with it for a number of years and who are deceased, retired, or near the retirement age.

Half of the sketches are biographies and half autobiographies. Thanks are due to Revs. T. E. Durham, J. W. Crowder, E. C. Routh, Frederick Eby, L. R. Elliott and Perry Evans for writing the biographies respectively of Drs. Ball, Carroll, Gambrell, Newman, Ray and Scarborough. They have done this as a labor of love.

Thanks also are due to the various publishers who have given permission to quote from their books, and to the various friends who have given information, encouragement and assistance at every stage of the work. May the book be a credit to the persons included and a help to the readers.

J. M. Price

Seminary Hill, Fort Worth, Texas

INTRODUCTION

Biography is history embodied in pulsating life. The events which compose historical records are never fully understandable when detached from persons. They become intelligible and thrilling when we interpret them in relation to the human agents who have set them in motion. Neither can the basic principles underneath the facts of history be effectively demonstrated until enshrined in the lives of those who have made it. History would be immeasurable impoverished—indeed would not exist—without biography.

It is such a conviction which has inspired the publication of this volume consisting of biography and autobiography. In and through the lives of the twelve men presented, we may read the history of one of the most important periods in Southern Baptist annals.

Further, we not only view a period; we also find the secret of a strategic institution, Southwestern Baptist Theological seminary. Every one of these men has made distinctly enriching contributions to the origination, the growth, the present stage of achievement, and future progress of this institution. We cannot adequately appraise them apart from the Seminary, or the Seminary apart from them. The two are united in sacred bonds which cannot be broken.

This volume not only makes available the inspiring facts of biography and autobiography; it also supplies a key sermon or address revelatory of the best emphasis and thinking of these noble workmen, so zealous in their devotion to the will of the Lord. This makes the book factual, personal, and inspiring.

Dr. J. M. Price has rendered invaluable service in assembling and editing the materials herein contained. To him, and all who have brought it to realization, our heartiest congratulations and gratitude.

We shall never cease being thankful for the privilege of personal acquaintance with the men who are the subjects of the various chapters. They have been and are the source of immeasurable blessings to us personally, as they have been, and will continue to be, to uncounted individuals, living on through them for all time to come.

E. D. Head, President
Southwestern Baptist Theological Seminary
Fort Worth, Texas

CHAPTER I

CHARLES T. BALL

BIOGRAPHICAL SKETCH*

Charles Thomas Ball, clergyman, educator, author, lecturer and dynamic leader in the field of education, was born in Oxford, North Carolina, February 3, 1866. He received his basic education in the public schools of North Carolina, an A. B. from Wake Forest College in 1898, and the Th.M. from the Southern Baptist Theological Seminary in 1903. He married Mary Agnes Peterson of Winston-Salem, North Carolina, November 30, 1897, and to this union two children were born, Marie Elizabeth and Charles E. Ball, M.D.

He became the dean of the Bible Department of Simmons College, now Hardin-Simmons University, in 1904 and served through 1911. He moved to Fort Worth, Texas, and became professor of Comparative Religion and Missions in the Southwestern Baptist Theological Seminary, heading that department from 1911 through 1919. He inaugurated the Extension Work of the Seminary and directed it in connection with the Missions Department. He organized the Baptist Student Missionary Movement in 1912, and directed its activities through 1919, promoting the movement throughout the South. He became the Executive Secretary of the American Baptist Student Union in 1920 and did a noble work with and for students throughout the nation for about five years.

Dr. Ball entered the pastorate of the Winsinoming Baptist Church of Philadelphia, Pennsylvania, in 1925, and rendered valuable service there. While pastor of this great church he turned his dynamic energies toward the establishment of a Baptist seminary in the city of brotherly love, Philadelphia. The

*By Rev. T. E. Durham, Pastor Arlington Heights Baptist Church, Fort Worth, Texas

Baptists of that city followed his leadership in raising funds to build a great school, the Eastern Baptist Theological Seminary, and made him its first President in 1925. He raised large sums of money for its operation, and a million dollars endowment for its security. He selected a strong faculty and started a great school.

He had in his heart to establish a great university and turned his energies toward building such a school in Philadelphia. He had enough encouragement to give up the presidency of the Seminary and give his full time to establishing the Eastern University in 1926. He selected a faculty, secured buildings and began work, putting in a large extension department. However, he did not get the support from the city which he felt that his school was entitled to.

So when he received support and encouragement from Arlington, Virginia, to establish a university there, he moved the Eastern University from Philadelphia to Arlington in 1936 and it became the Arlington University. It was incorporated and chartered by the laws of Virginia. The school was growing and making splendid progress when Mrs. Ball became very ill, requiring much of his time and attention. His office sent out thousands of catalogues to ministers of all faiths in America and in England. With long experience he had made a strong university extension department, having students enrolled from this country and from England. His age and Mrs. Ball's illness clouded his greatest dream, namely, "a university near our Nation's Capitol, serving the English speaking world."

He was a thorough teacher, gifted in organizing preachers and students for effective achievements for the Master's cause. He was a tireless worker, preaching, teaching and lecturing. He was a writer of no mean ability. He has many laurels in his crown of achievement which will last for the ages to come. The Bible Department in Simmons College has become one of the honored Bible departments of our southwest. The department of Comparative Religion and Missions in the Southwestern Seminary encircles the earth with its influence, by its missionaries preaching and teaching the pure gospel of the Lord Jesus Christ to a needy world.

The Eastern Baptist Seminary has grown to be a strong

school, with a large endowment, receiving ample Northern Baptist support, with a recognized faculty of scholars, serving a large student body from this nation and other lands. The Baptist Student Missionary Movement was the forerunner of the Baptist Student Union which is one of our most influential agencies. It held effective national conventions both in Fort Worth, Texas, and Louisville, Kentucky, published a magazine and supported Dr. and Mrs. A. L. Aulick as field workers.

He was a good husband and a faithful father, providing well for his household. Mrs. Mary Agnes Ball was a devoted helpmeet to her gifted husband. She was a great Christian, a good mother, and an understanding, helpful neighbor, was an A.B. graduate of Salem College, Winston-Salem, North Carolina. She died May 10, 1943, after a long illness. Marie Elizabeth Ball, the only daughter, died at an early age. Dr. Charles Edward Ball, the only son, after attending Simmons and Baylor graduated at Jefferson Medical College, Philadelphia, and has grown to be a famous physician, an eye, ear, nose and throat specialist. Dr. Ball passed away on January 26, 1943. May he yet speak through his sermons for many years to come, and the Lord inspire the readers.

THE CROSS, SATAN'S HOUR AND THE POWER OF DARKNESS*

The text is Matt. 27:45,46. "Now from the sixth hour there was darkness over all the land until the ninth hour. And about the ninth hour Jesus cried with a loud voice saying, 'Eli, Eli, lama sabachthani, that is, 'My God, my God, why hast thou forsaken me?' "

Jesus went on the cross at nine o'clock in the morning, which was the sixth hour. There were three hours of day-light, in which there was gambling at the foot of the cross. Taunts, also, and insults were cast at Him by those who were passing, and a number of other happenings, including the seven words spoken by our Lord to those about Him. The darkness came at noon and lasted until the ninth hour, which was three o'clock in the afternoon.

It is my purpose at this time to undertake to give you a spiritual interpretation of the sufferings of our Lord and Master on the Cross. It is not my purpose to discuss His physical sufferings. Physical suffering and physical death were involved. They did drive nails through His hands and through His feet, and there was loss of blood and great bodily physical suffering; but in this discussion I am giving small attention to these because it is my conviction that our Lord thought very little about them.

In the garden our Lord prayed three times, "My Father, if it be possible let this cup pass from me. Nevertheless, not as I will, but as thou wilt." He knew that on the morrow He must meet in a death battle on the spiritual plane, during three hours of the densest darkness, the Old Serpent, Satan, the Devil, and solve for man and for God the problem of sin. This was a spiritual and not a physical conflict. But inquires one, "Was it not looking forward to and shrinking from suffering on the Cross and caused our Lord to pray in the Garden of Gethsemane, and sweat great drops of blood?" No, I cannot accept that view.

Our Lord suffered great agony in the garden the evening

*From *The Victorious Christ* by Charles T. Ball, American Publishing Co.

before the crucifixon and prayed three times to His father to deliver Him if in accordance with His will, because He knew that on the morrow He would face spiritual death, and actually die the second death, which means Hell and separation from God. He not only died the second death but went to Hell (Hades) for each of us. This He did in our stead.

Did you ever see God at His best? It has been said, and I think well, that all departments of nature sometime, somewhere, come to their highest and best expression. For example the highest and best expression of the vegetable kingdom is a full-blown rose; the highest and best expression of the mineral kingdom is a crystal of carbon; the highest and the best expression of animal nature is a well-bred horse; the highest and the best expression of Deity is a Man nailed to a Cross. Did you ever see God at His best? If you ever did, you saw a Man nailed to a Cross, by the eye of faith.

I wish to bring to you a few definite thoughts of this text that you can take home with you and remember and, I hope, profit by them.

First, it was a cry from the heart and lips of One who had had Himself put on the Cross to die under direct command from God the Father. John 16:17,18: "Therefore doth the Father love me, because I lay down my life that I might take it again. No one taketh it away from me, but I lay it down of myself. I have power to lay it down and I have power to take it again. The commandment received I from My Father."

Sometime, somewhere, back in the councils of eternity, before times eternal, God issued a command to His son to die for a lost world. True, there were men who thought they killed Him and the Devil did kill Him. But really and truly His death was the voluntary offering of Himself as a sacrifice for our sins. He did not die to make it possible for God to love lost sinners: for God loved them already so much that He commanded His only begotten Son to die for them. But He did die in order to make it right for God to save sinners. Scriptures put it in Romans 3:25,26: "Whom God set forth to be a propitiation, through faith in His blood, to show His righteousness at this present season; the showing, I say, of his righteousness at this present season; that He might Himself be just, and the justifier of Him that hath faith in Jesus Christ."

Second, it was a cry from the heart and lips of One who when He uttered it was being "made sin for us." II Cor. 5:21: "Him who knew no sin He made to be sin on our behalf, that we might become the righteousness of God in Him." This Scripture means and says that it was God the Father who put Jesus on the Cross. It was God the Father who "made Him to be sin." What does it mean? This is a great mystery. It means, in part at least, that the sinless Christ stepped into my shoes and took the responsibility for my sins. He became responsible to God in my stead.

Third, it was a cry from the heart and lips of One, who when He uttered it was tasting death for every man. (Hebrews 2:9). What do I mean by this? I mean that if you are His He was doing your dying, and left no dying for you to do. The death which Jesus died on the Cross for each of us was what the Bible sometimes calls the second death. It means Hell and eternal separation from God. This is why I say that when our Lord uttered this cry He was doing our dying and did not leave the smallest particle for us to do. If you are His, death, can never come near you, nor touch you.

Fourth, it was a cry from the heart and lips of One, who when He uttered it was overwhelmed in the mystery of doubt. Yes, He said, "Why" one time; but they were not His "doubts" nor His "whys." When He stepped into our shoes and took our place under the law He became responsible to God for our sins, and it was in this situation that He gave expression to our "doubts" and "whys." And because Jesus said "why" for us, because He mingled His voice with ours, God will hear when we say "why" and quiet our doubts and fears.

Fifth, it was a cry from the heart and from the lips of One, who when He uttered it was overwhelmed in the mystery of silence. It is noticeable and most amazing that after our Lord went on the Cross, no word came to Him from home. The Heavens were brass above His head.

It was easy enough for our Lord to hear from home before He went on the Cross. At His birth myriads of angels appeared on the scene. They had come from Heaven to celebrate this great event. They sang the songs He had heard in heaven around the throne. At His baptism the Holy Spirit appeared in the form of a dove to denote that the Spirit would be upon Him in all His fulness for His life work. The voice of the Father was also heard: "This is my beloved Son, in whom I am well pleased." On the mount of transfiguration the heavenly visitors, Moses and Elijah, appeared, and the voice of God was heard again saying: "This is my beloved Son, hear ye Him." And I believe that many times when our Lord was praying in the silent hours of the night and all alone, He heard the voice of His Father speaking to Him, and I doubt not that many times there were heavenly visitors.

Why this awful, dreadful silence in the hour when He most needed sympathy and when He was most misunderstood? It was because this One was as much man as if He had not been God, and at the same time as much God as if He had not been man, this One, the God-man, must of necessity perform this service for God and for man all alone.

Man could not help because of his guilt. He had sinned and lost his standing before God, and it was for him, it was to restore him, that the God-man was dying. God could not help because it was His holiness that had been outraged by man's sins. It must be done by One who represented both God and man and who was both God and man. Hence the silence! No word from Heaven, no help from man.

Sixth, it was a cry from the heart and lips of One, who when He uttered it was overwhelmed in the mystery of darkness. I believe this was the densest darkness this world will ever know. It was the darkest of the pit. It was the picture God gave of the sin that had put Jesus on the Cross.

No man saw the major sufferings of Jesus. The dense darkness concealed these evidences of suffering. The Scriptures tell us that it covered "all the land." Suffice it to say that it was Hell's hour and the power of darkness and the densest darkness the universe will ever know: the darkness of Hell!.

Seventh, it was a cry from the heart and lips of One who when He uttered it was fathoming the deepest abyss of sorrow. What is sorrow, anyhow? Did you ever try to analyze it? Someone has said that sorrow is the lack of something. The sorrowing soul lacks something that is necessary to its happiness.

As a pastor, I stood on one occasion with a young married couple before a little white casket which contained the body of thier first-born. They were sorrowing because they loved the child; it had gone from them.

Did our Lord lack something? When He was being "made sin" did God the Father turn from His dying Son? Was there a break in that high and holy fellowship that had never known a shock? Did it mean that God could not have fellowship with His own Son when He was being made sin? Did God turn from Him at this moment and did our Lord become conscious that He was "forsaken" even by His Father? "My God, my God, why hast thou forsaken me?"

When our Lord stood in our stead and took upon Himself the responsibility for our sins this act separated Him from God. When He uttered this cry He was experiencing the very worst there is in separation.

Eighth, it was a cry from the heart and lips of One, who when He uttered it was dying a death-destroying death. The Lord Jesus knew when He went on the Cross He would put death out of business. The apostle Paul bears record of this great fact in Second Timothy 1:10: "Our Saviour Jesus Christ, who abolished death and brought life and immortality to light through the gospel."

Not only did He abolish death, but destroyed the one through whom death came into the world. Hebrews 2:14: "Since the children are sharers in flesh and blood, He also, in like manner, partook of the same; that through death He might bring to naught him that had the power of death, that is, the Devil." Our Lord Jesus Christ partook of our nature, flesh, and blood, which involved death. This He did voluntarily for our sakes. He knew that He was stepping into the realm of death when He laid aside temporarily some of the privileges of Deity, emptied Himself, as told in Phil. 2:7,8. Our Lord's death was a voluntary act, a high and holy submission that Satan might slay Him. He knew all this was to be, and that it would fulfill the demands of the spiritual second death.

It was in this voluntary act of submission that He became our substitute, and this is what gives value to His death, which value He transfers to us and God accepts. He stood in our stead and experiences the second death for us. It was the knowledge that this would take place on the morrow that brought bloody sweat and great agony as He prayed the evening before in the garden. And it was the knowledge on His part that this act would save us from Hell and the Second Death that put joy in His sufferings. Our salvation was His joy in the midst of this suffering and death.

Now, since what I have said is true, and I believe in accordance with the teachings of the Scriptures, there are three great words with deep meaning that I must pronounce to you.

First, the death of our Lord was and is and will forever be, a vicarious death. He suffered and died the second death in our stead. He descended into the lower regions, that is into Hades, and came back for us. He rose from the grave also and ascended to the right hand of the Father for us.

Isaiah 53 is a great commentary on the vicariousness of the death of our Lord. We find in that great chapter the following expressions: "He was bruised for our iniquities;" "Jehovah hath laid on Him the iniquity of us all;" "When thou shalt make His soul an offering for sin;" "and He shall bear our iniquities." This great doctrine of substitution is found throughout the Scriptures. His death was vicarious. He died for our sins and in our stead.

Second, His death was atoning. He made atonement for our sins. Our Lord was the greatest bridge builder of the universe. He bridged with His own person the deep and yawning chasm that separated men from God. Jesus did not die to cause God to love lost sinners but rather God commanded Him to die. "God is love," the Scriptures tell us, but God is also justice, and He must have a just cause for saving before any man could be saved. God, as God the Father, could not go on the cross to die because He was the One whose holiness had been outraged by sin. No mere man could go on the cross and die and make atonement because it was man who had sinned. There must be one who represented both God and man; one who was as much God as if He had not been man. This One must make the atonement.

Let me call your attention again to this great Scripture found in Romans 3:25,26: "Whom God set forth to be a propitiation through faith, in His blood, to show His righteousness because of the passing over of the sins done beforetime, in the forbearance of God; for the showing, I say, of His righteousness at this present season; that He might Himself be just; and the justifier of Him that hath faith in Jesus."

A good Scotch woman lay dying. The Christian doctor knew that all the children could reach her bedside while she was still alive except the oldest daughter. She was too far away. After she had given her blessing to all the children present, the suggestion was made that she be asked whether or not she had a message to leave for Mary, who would probably reach home after her mother had gone. In her weakness the mother replied, "Yes, if I am gone when Mary arrives, tell her that the Bridge holds." Yes, it will hold for each of us also. Our Lord Jesus was the architect and the builder. The bridge will hold. He is the bridge. His death was an atoning death.

Third, His death was, and is, and always will be an expiatory death. It means that Jesus made expiation for our sins. Propitiation is a great New Testament word. Propitiate means "to satisfy, to appease, to purify."

Expiate, an Old Testament word, is a much stronger word. It means "to extinguish, put out of existence." So let us hold to our word expiate. The death of Christ was an expiatory death. On the Cross He expiated our sins; He extinguished them. He made them not to be; He put them out of existence.

In the Scriptures, in many places where God is spoken of as dealing with our sins, we find such expressions as:

Isaiah 44:22—"I have blotted out, as a thick-cloud, thy transgressions, and as a cloud, thy sins; return unto Me; for I have redeemed thee."

Isaiah 38:17—"Thou hast cast all my sins behind Thy back."

Psalms 103:12—"As far as the east is from the west, so far hath He removed our transgressions from us."

Micah 7:19—"Thou wilt cast all their sins into the depths of the sea."

Finally God says, Hebrews 8:12. "And their sins will I remember no more."

All the above can mean nothing less than that God chooses to put our sins out of His mind; not to remember our sins against us when, through Christ, we have become His own. That is, God chooses to forget our sins. A dying preacher said he could not make Christ remember that he had ever committed sin. Christ died to put away our sin. Praise His Holy Name.!

CHAPTER II

W. W. BARNES

AUTOBIOGRAPHICAL SKETCH

I was born February 28, 1883, in the village of Tiosnot (Elm City), formerly in Edgecombe, now in Wilson County, N.C. My father's and mother's people came from England to Isle of Wight County, Virginia, within a half-century after Jamestown was settled. For nearly a century they were active in the colony—members of the colonial legislature and the Governor's Council. They were members of the Church of England. Some, under the influence of the Great Awakening, became Baptists and left Virginia to settle in the new county of Edgecombe. Some were members of the Baptist church that left Isle of Wight in 1742 and settled where Scotland Neck now is.

My father was a physician and farmer, educated in Cincinnati and New York. He died when I was thirteen. Under the influence of a Missionary Baptist preacher, Elder Mark Bennett, my mother's grand-parents took the missionary side when the division occured in the 1830's. Most of her relatives took the anti-missionary side. Under the influence of Elder Bennett two of mother's aunts were sent to Chowan College in the 1850's. In due course mother went to Chowan, graduating in 1871. Since ladies did not speak in public, mother listened to her graduation address ("Hope") read by President W. M. Wingate of Wake Forest College. I have the address in her hand-writing.

My ancesters for eight or nine generations have been Baptists. Father's ancestor, Elder Jonathan Thomas, founded the church, known as Toisnot, now Wilson, in 1756. Mother had five great uncles who were preachers. Baptisticism is deeply ingrained in my blood. I became a Sunday school member the

17

first Sunday in January, 1894. The church had seventy-seven members; the Sunday School averaged about sixty. The Rev. Q. C. Davis, father of Professor W. H. Davis of the Southern Seminary, had just resigned the pastorate and the son had just left the class. Mr. John Friend was the teacher. He was well named.

I revelled in the new atmosphere. The Sunday school lessons were studied daily with avidity. I joined the church during a revival and was baptized October 16, 1898 by the pastor, the Rev. M. L. Kesler. They made me a teacher in the spring of 1899 and superintendent in the fall. I served also as janitor (without wages), and led the singing. Later this church was my first pastorate. In fact, I functioned in every capacity except president of the Woman's Missionary Society. They never risked me in that place.

My formal education began in the country one-room school and was continued in the village school, supplemented by a private school, thus giving a school year of nine months. My real education was given me by my mother. She taught me mathematics (favorite in those years), English, Latin, and French. In my sixteenth and seventeenth years we read Church History together. Her volume is before me as I write on Wednesday, 18 June, 1947. (On Wednesday, 18 June, 1913, I came to Fort Worth to accept the Professorship of Church History. For these thirty-four years I have tried to interpret Church History in the light of her teachings.)

In August, 1900, I was licensed by the Elm City Church and entered Wake Forest College three weeks later. My college career was not particularly notable. Most of the time was given to study. Perhaps more should have been given to athletics and the literary society. I was fortunate in not having the multitudinous organizations that distract students today. The degrees of Bachelor of Arts and Master of Arts were received in 1904. Thirty years later, at the centennial celebration, the College conferred the Doctorate of Divinity.

The first year out of college I was tutor of the children of two American families near Santiago de Cuba, and the following year principal of a public school in my home county. There were three of us teaching—the daughter of a Primitive Baptist

preacher, the daughter of a Freewill Baptist deacon and myself. We had frank and friendly discussions but no friction in
school administration or religion. I was also pastor of my home
church and of the church in Fremont, in the adjoining county
to the south—two Sundays at each church.

In the fall of 1906 I entered the Southern Seminary at Louisville. I was fortunate in both college and seminary in having
faculties of experience and wisdom. A few years after I left
each school the faculties began to break up through death or
retirement. I am grateful to a kind Providence for my opportunity in each school.

In February, 1909, I received the degree of Master in Theology from the Seminary and went to Havana, Cuba, to take
charge of the Cuban-American College under the Home Mission Board. My duties were: to have direction of the school,
teach the class of young ministers, and preach in English Sunday morning. My spare time was taken in assisting Dr. M. N.
McCall in directing the mission work. Among the leaders of
the Cuban work today are some of the ministers I taught then.
Unavoidable circumstances led me to resign in May, 1912.

I returned to Louisville and completed graduate work with
a major in Church History and minors in Hebrew and Sociology. On the day of graduation with the degree of Doctor of
Theology came the inquiry concerning my advailibility for the
Chair of Church History in Southwestern. Two days later
the position was offered me. I held that Chair from 1913 to
1946, when I was transferred to the Research Professorship in
Baptist History, a new chair in Baptist history. In preparation
for this work I spent the calendar year, 1919, in Columbia, University majoring in American History, and much time since
studying American secular and Christian history.

My experience of life, both as it has come and in retrospect,
confirms me in the truth received from my mother that God's
providence is sure.

A RELIGION ADEQUATE FOR TODAY*

John 14:6, "I am the way, the truth, and the life."

Man is a religious creature. The philosopher and man of letters, Ernest Renan, is quoted as saying "Man is incurably religious." This dictum of the unbelieving philosopher is proved to be correct by research into the life of all the peoples of the earth—the most highly civilized and the lowest in the stages of civilization. This being true, what sort of religion ought man to have? An adequate religion must satisfy man as he looks at the past; as he lives in present; as he faces the future. Such a religion must do four things for man.

I. As man looks at the past his religion must furnish to his intellect a reasonable explanation of the universe in which he lives.

Man's intellectual life is an important phase of his being. He must realize this even in his religious outlook. His theology is the result of his effort to rationalize the truths presented by his religion. In every religion, however naive and simple in its forms, there must be a sense of satisfaction concerning the world around us and the heavens above us. In the history of the religions of man there are many oddities, some of them downright foolish, in the explanations of the universe. In the religions of the ancient world—Babylonia, Assyria, Egypt, Greece, and Rome; among the Aborigines in North and South America; among the primitive peoples of Africa and Asia—in all of these there are found efforts to explain the universe. Among the intellectuals of Europe and America today there are efforts at such explanation. Some would explain the universe —its origin and its control—in terms of blind chance, materialistic fatalism. Others see a spiritual reality that furnishes an adequate answer to "the problem of the universe."

Christianity has its historical basis in the revelation in the Bible. There must be a starting point. The Bible begins with a statement magnificient in its simplicity: "In the beginning God." This starting point, when once it grips man's thought, is the answer to life's problems. The apostle puts his finger

*Radio address over KFJZ, Fort Worth, Texas, February 2, 1947

upon this fundamental principle when he said to King Agrippa: "'Why is it judged incredible with you if God doth raise the dead?" Given belief in God, any question of life, even the question of death, is answered.

The same apostle in another place sounds the depth of human thinking and reaches the height of intellectual achievement when he says: "For in him were all things created, in the heavens and upon the earth, things visible and things invisible, whether thrones or dominions or principalities or powers: all things have been created through him, and unto him; and he is before all things, and in him all things consist." (Colossians 1:16-17). If you, through that insight into reality called faith, have grasped that fundamental truth enunciated by Paul that there is One who stands at the center of this universe, who is the Author of its being and who controls its destiny, you can face a world torn to shreds. You can face your own small world going to pieces. The apostle was in a Roman prison facing the possibility of death by a Roman sword when he wrote those words just quoted. What did Rome matter? What mattered Roman soldiers and Roman prisons? Yea, what mattered death from a Roman sword when Paul knew Him who made all things and holds all things together?

II. Not only must a religion, to be adequate, furnish an explanation of the origin of the universe, but an adequate religion must furnish a sufficient moral guide for the present.

Man's need is primarily moral. His material resources may be limited, but if his moral values are clear and adequate, he is a man. An adequate religion must hold forth before man a high moral standard. Man never rises higher than his moral ideal, and those ideals must be buttressed by religion. In the history of nations their downgrade may be traced to a breakdown of their moral ideals which have weakened because their religious underpinning has given way. The Bible is *par excellance,* a Book of religion. Any history or geography or science included in the Bible is incidental to the moral development shown therein. Men have somtimes puzzled themselves over what they consider low moral standards and practices in the Old Testament, but I would remind you that the Christian re-

ligion comes to flower in the progressive revelation culminating
in the New Testament. "God, having of old time spoken unto
the fathers in the prophets by divers portions and in divers
manners, hath at the end of these days spoken unto us in his
Son, whom he appointed heir of all things, through whom also
he made the worlds; who being the effulgence of his glory,
and the very image of his substance, and upholding all things
by the word of his power, when he had made purification of
sins, sat down on the right hand of the Majesty on high."
(Hebrews 1:1-3).

The Bible furnishes a moral guide to man floundering in
his uncertainty. Man's chief difficulties with the Bible are not
intellectual, but moral. When I see a man who is losing his
grasp on spiritual, religious realities and places the cause there-
for in his intellectual doubts concerning something he sees in
the Bible, I know his moral foundations are giving way. I have
seen the proof of this in many instances. He begins to slip
morally. The Bible condemns his acts. He seeks to justify
himself, to escape condemnation, by denying the truth of the
Book which condemns his manner of life. He reads the Bible,
or hears it read, and has a sense of obligation to a certain task.
He is not willing to give himself to the task. He endeavors to
by-pass the duty by denying the authority of Him who imposes
the duty. He has his "doubts about the Bible."

Christianity, above all the religions in the history of man,
puts before you and me a high moral standard and a perfect
moral guide. For centuries men have paid their respect to
Jesus of Nazareth. Christian, Jew and Pagan have recognized
his moral perfection. For many years a great American daily
paper has published an editorial tribute to Him at Christmas
time. Last Christmas one of our Fort Worth daily papers
published this editorial from the other daily. The French philosopher, Renan, whom I quoted at the beginning, paid his tribute by writing a volume dealing with Jesus. Many years ago
a Jewish friend of mine, a man learned in eight languages, ancient and modern, assured me that he was so enamored with
Jesus of Nazareth and His teachings that he read the Gospel
stories each day in four or five languages in order that he
might get every angle or phase of thought in Jesus' parables.

Some of Jesus' opponents testified that no man ever spake like this man.

The New Testament, in the Gospels and in the interpretations of Jesus given in the other books, holds before men of the first century and of all succeeding centuries the high moral ideal illustrated in the life and teachings of Jesus. No man ever went astray who seriously made Jesus his guide. I am not concerned about a man's theology, about his scientific opinions, about his economic theories, about any of his intellectual vagaries and outlooks, if he sincerely takes Jesus of Nazareth as his moral standard and guide. Christianity alone, among all the religions of the world, furnishes a guide to duty.

III. In the third place, an adequate religion must furnish for the present strength to perform one's duty to God and man.

Many a great thinker has left on record high thoughts concerning man and his relations and obligations to the Supreme Being and his relations and obligations to his fellow man. Marcus Aurelius, the Roman Emperor, has left us essays that point upward. Many religious teachers, founders of and leaders in some of the great religions of the world, have left us great teachings. Some of these teachings approximate teachings of Jesus, but none of these have been able in their own lives to illustrate their great ideals nor to inspire in their followers any great effort to achieve.

Study the record of Jesus as given us in the Gospels. Somehow he was able to touch the life of a tax-collector and make him fit to be a member of the apostolic band. He could call unknown fishermen from their boats and inspire them to go forth and win a hostile world, not afraid to stand before governors and kings. He could inspire a fallen woman, a social outcast, to new ideals and efforts at living. He could take the profane fisherman, Simon, and send him on a career of world-conquering fame. Did you ever notice the Gospel reference to the eye of Jesus? He must have had a penetrating eye. How many times reference is made to the fact that He looked at someone! He looked at the rich young man and saw his love of money. He put His finger on the sensitive spot in his soul. May we hope that the young man in after time was lifted up by that look! He looked at Nathanael and saw an Israelite in whom was no guile. And all of Nathanael's doubts fled. He looked at Peter who had just denied Him. The look crushed Peter and prepared him to see the risen Christ on Sunday following.

The apostle says, "I can do all things through Christ who strengtheneth me." That has been the experience of multitudes. Many a youth in whom man has seen little promise has become a William Carey, a David Livingstone. Millions whom the world has never recognized have received the inspiration and strength to meet life faithfully. Many of the men and women who have made our country great have found their source of strength and inspiration in Jesus of Nazareth.

Even beyond the bounds of organized Christianity much service to humanity has found its inspiration and its will to do in the life and teachings of Jesus. There were no orphanages, hospitals, or other houses for the care of man until He came. We have among us a great relief organization that serves the world in war and in peace that receives its very name from the cross of Jesus.

IV. An adequate religion must satisfy the intellectual craving for a tolerable explanation of the origin and continuance of the universe; must constitute a sufficient moral guide and give strength to perform the duties of the present life; so, also, in the fourth place, an adequate religion must give assurance for the future.

We are familiar today with the several security programs— the efforts of the political authorities in state and nation to give assurance for the future. The religious bodies of the United States have been hastened in their programs of security for their workers by the comparable efforts of the secular authorities. May I respectfully remind you that all of these efforts are based on secular and material foundations. The dollar bill that you have is not value in itself. It is a promise on the part of the United States government to pay the bearer on demand a silver dollar. That piece of paper, therefore, is of no more value than is the credit of the United States government. And we know from history, past and current, that nations rise and fall, they come and go. And those of us whose memories reach back fifteen years know how quickly material values fall and how helpless political governments are in the premises.

When I was a youth of twenty-one, the first year I was out
of college (1904), I was tutor of the children of two American
families in eastern Cuba. We lived ten miles north of Santiago,
in the village of Dos Bocas, on the railroad between Havana
and Santiago. The railroad, the river and the highway ran
parallel to one another, following the winding valley between the
two mountain ridges. Our home was situated up the mountain
side, looking across the valley toward the west. The front yard
was a beautiful flower garden. It was built up thirty feet above
the river, supported by a massive stone wall. A stairway led
down to a foot-bridge. Beyond the river, about twenty-five
acres were planted in all manner of tropical fruits.

In the afternoon I used to watch the sun go down behind
the ridge on the other side of the valley. The ridge was
bordered by a fringe of bamboo that resembled a lace curtain
up-right. By four o'clock the sun touched the bamboo fringe
and slowly disappeared behind the curtain. Day after day, as
I watched the approaching sunset, counting the minutes as the
sun moved down the width of the bamboo, I resolved to go
up the ridge some day to learn if I could see beyond the sunset.

One afternoon in October, as the sun touched the fringe
atop the ridge, I sprang from my seat on the porch, hastened
down the stone steps, across the bridge, through the orchard,
across the highway and the railroad and up the path that
wound like a thread up the mountain side. I looked back toward
the residence. Night had settled in the valley—there is no twi-
light in the tropics—and was gradually reaching up the side
of the mountain, approaching the residence.

As I reached the bamboo fringe and pushed through, a vision
opened before me that has cheered me along the road for these
four decades and more. Behind me was the valley of darkness,
enveloping the place where I lived, whence I had just witnessed
the set of the sun. Before me I saw the sun in all his brilliance
shining up on a plain about ten miles wide. Magnificent royal
palms dotted the landscape, hundreds of head of cattle were
grazing on the luscious grass, millions of tropical flowers cast a
riot of color, swarms of bees were extracting nectar. Beauty,
abundance and peace reigned in every direction.

A lesson stamped itself upon my soul that afternoon and a-bides with me today. The day passes noontide and the shadows lengthen toward the east. We look at the path of life approaching the western horizon. The valley behind is filling with darkness; ahead are the light, the beauty, the abounding joy of eternal day. At eventide there shall be light.

Christianity looks to the future with assurance. Confucianism looks back to its founder; the glory of Buddhism is in the past; Mohammedanism had no higher word than that given by its leader a dozen centuries ago. Even Judaism has no message for the future. She looks back to Moses and endeavors to meet the present as well as possible. The Golden Age of Christianity is yet to be. Lord Tennyson looks forward to

"That far-off divine event
Toward which the whole creation moves."

William Cullen Bryant, watching a water-fowl wind its sure way through the unchartered skies, received a lesson for himself.

"He who from zone to zone
Guides through the boundless sky thy certain flight
In the long way that I must tread alone
Will lead my steps aright."

May I read you quotations from two philosophies of life that illustrate what I mean? There is a poem by Omar Khayyam, from ancient Persia, translated by Edward Fitzgerald. Two stanzas read as follows:

"We are no other than a moving row
Of Magic-Shadow shapes that come and go
Round with the Sun-illumined Lantern held
In Midnight by the Master of the Show.

And that inverted Bowl they call the Sky,
Whereunder crawling cooped we live and die,
Lift not your hands to *It* for help—for It
As importently moves as you or I."

On the other hand listen to these words from James Russell Lowell:

"Truth forever on the scaffold,
Wrong forever on the throne;

Yet that scaffold sways the future,
And behind the dim unknown,
Standeth God within the shadow
Keeping watch above His own."

But one greater than all these poets that I have quoted,
as he faced certain death, wrote: "I know whom I have believed
and am persuaded that he is able to guard that which I have
committed to him against that day." The apostle Paul wrote
these words to his young fellow-laborer, Timothy, laid down
his pen on the table and his head upon the Roman block and
stepped out into eternity with assurance.

CHAPTER III

B. H. CARROLL

BIOGRAPHICAL SKETCH*

Benajah Harvey Carroll, of Irish descent, was born on a farm near Carrolton in Carroll County, Mississippi, December 27, 1843. He was the fifth son and seventh child in a family of twelve children. At seven he moved with the family to Arkansas, near Monticello and spent seven years more on a farm. He enjoyed fishing, hunting, and adventure. He delighted in story-telling and playing pranks.

In the fall of 1858 he moved with the family to Burleson County, Texas. Little is known of his early schooling, but it is known that he attended school at Monticello, Arkansas, and Caldwell, Texas. From his early life on he was an incessant reader. He said he began to read history at the age of four He was always a student. As a boy he taught school, and made the reputation then of being a born teacher.

In 1859, in his sixteenth year, he went to Baylor University at Old Independence. He was in Baylor less than two years and made a wonderful record as a student and debater. His speech on the campus of Baylor against the secession of Texas from the Union was a classic. His reading covered every branch of learning and his memory was most astounding. He averaged reading three hundred pages a day for more than fifty years, and often quoted from memory what he had not seen for forty years.

In 1861 he mustered into the Confederate Service at San Antonio, as a Texas Ranger, which service lasted one year and was filled with dangerous and thrilling adventures. In 1862 he joined the Seventeenth Regiment of the Texas Infantry at Aus-

*By Prof. J. W. Crowder, formerly Professor of English Bible, Southwestern Baptist Seminary.

tin. He served through the War and was severely wounded
in the battle of Mansfield, Louisiana. He was highly com-
mended by Colonel Allen for his courage, bravery, courtesy,
and defense of the right. In the meantime he made some most
remarkable war speeches and held some notable camp debates.
In all his debates he took the more unlikely side, and always
won.

In this four-year war period his infidelity had full sway, but
he was converted in a Methodist Camp-Meeting in the summer
of 1865. He was licensed to preach in 1866, and in November
of the same year was ordained. On December 28 following, he
was happily married to Miss Ellen Bell. To this marriage
several children were born, three of whom are now living;
Charles, a retired teacher and preacher, Katherine, a missionary,
and Annie Louise. It proved to be a God-made match. She
was a beautiful, loyal, devoted wife, mother, and Christian.
After the death of his first wife, he married Miss Hallie Harrison, daughter of General Thomas Harrison, of Waco, Texas.
To this union one son, Francis Harrison Carroll, was born. He
is now a news columnist in California.

Immediately following his ordination, Dr. Carroll entered
upon a most eventful and meaningful ministry. His first attempt was a combination of preaching and teaching, a failure
financially but a success otherwise. He then tried preaching
and farming, another failure financially. Then he said, "Come
weal or woe, I shall give my life wholly to preaching the Gospel." This he did, and in 1870 he was called as assistant pastor of the First Baptist Church of Waco, and on January 1,
1871, he became full pastor. Thus he began a most remarkable
pastorate, which continued twenty-eight years.

During his arduous pastoral work Dr. Carroll was outstanding as a denominational leader and champion of civic righteousness. His speeches and sermons did much to establish these
causes. He was a commanding figure in the Texas and Southern Baptist Conventions, being six feet, four inches tall and very
handsome. He standardized Baptist orthodoxy in the South
and led many campaigns for righteousness and education, including the Prohibition Campaign in Texas in 1887, several for
the payment of debts on Baylor University, the State Mission

Board, and Southwestern Seminary.

One of the greatest characteristics of Dr. Carroll was his co-operation with all organized Baptist work. Some of his most notable addresses were: one before the Southern Baptist Convention at Richmond, Virginia, on "The Wisdom of Mission Work in Texas"; another before the National Education Society at Birmingham, Alabama, in 1891, on "The Needless Multiplication of Colleges"; and his Centennial Address before the Southern Baptist Convention at Atlanta, Georgia, on "Home Missions in America for One Hundred Years."

He held two religious debates. One was with Dr. O. Fisher, a Methodist Bishop, on "Christian Baptism", "Infant Baptism", and "The Baptism in the Holy Spirit", The other was with Dr. Wilmeth, a disciple of Alexander Campbell, on "The Order of Repentance and Faith", "The Design of Baptism", and "The Setting Up of the Kingdom."

The most monumental work of B. H. Carroll is the Southwestern Baptist Theological Seminary. Along with this should be noted his literary productions, including *Interpretation of the English Bible* (seventeen volumes), eighteen volumes of sermons and fifteen volumes of other material (yet unpublished), which constitute an invaluable, enduring Carroll library.

Dr. Carroll died November 11, 1914 and was buried in Waco, Texas. A while before his death he prayed that he might recover so as to preach just one more sermon. He was indeed, "the colossus of Baptist history."

MY INFIDELITY AND WHAT BECAME OF IT*

There was nothing in my home life to beget infidelity. My father was a self-educated Baptist minister, preaching to village or country churches. My mother was a devoted Christian of deep and humble piety. There were no infidel books in our home library, nor in any other accessible to me. My teachers were Christians—generally preachers. There were no infidels of my acquaintance, and no public sentiment in favor of them. My infidelity was never from without, but always from within.

From unrembered time this skepticism progressed irregularly. Sometimes in one hour there would be more progress in extent and definiteness than in previous months. These short periods of huge advances were always sudden and startling. Place and circumstances had but little to do with them. The doubt was seldom germane to the topic under consideration. At times it came when I was in the Sunday School or hearing a sermon or bowed with the others in family prayer—more frequently when waking at night after healthful sleep, and still more frequently when rambling alone in the fields or woods or mountain heights.

Thus, before I knew what infidelity was, I was an infidel. My child-mind was fascinated by strange and sometimes horrible questionings concerning many religious subjects. Long before I had read the experiences of others, I had been borne far beyond sight of any shore, wading and swimming beyond my depth after solutions to such questions as the "philosopher's stone," the "elixir of life," and "the fountain of youth," but mainly the "chief good."

I understand now much better the character and direction of the questionings of that early period. I know now that I never doubted the being, personality and government of God. I was never an atheist or pantheist. I never doubted the existence and ministry of angels—pure spirits never embodied: I could never have been a Sadducee. I never doubted the essential distinction between spirit and matter: I could never have been a materialist.

*Address before Ministers' Institute in Nashville, February, 1892.
From *Sermons* by B. H. Carroll, American Baptist Publication Society. Used by permission.

And as to the origin of things, the philosophy of Democritus, developed by Epicurus, more by Lucretius, and gone to seed in the unverified hypothesis of modern evolutionists—such a godless, materialistic anti-climax of philosophy never had the slightest attraction or temptation for me. The intuitions of humanity preserved me from any ambition to be descended from either beast or protoplasm. I never doubted the immortality of the soul and conscious future existence. I never doubted the final just judgment by the Creator of the world.

But my infidelity related to the Bible and its manifest doctrines. I doubted that it was God's book; an inspired revelation of His will to man. I doubted miracles, the divinity of Jesus, and his vicarious expiation for the sins of man. I doubted any real power and vitality in the Christian religion. I never doubted that the Scriptures claimed inspiration, nor that they taught unequivocally the divinity and vicarious expiation of Jesus.

The trifling expedient of accepting the Bible as "inspired in spots" never occured to me. To accept, with Renan, its natural parts and arbitrarily deny its supernatural, or to accept the book as from God, and then strike at its heart by a false interpretation that denied the divinity and vicarious expiation of Jesus —these were follies of which I was never guilty. What anybody wanted, in a religious way, with the shell after the kernel was gone I never could understand.

While the beginnings of my infidelity cannot be recalled, I can give the date when it took tangible shape. I do know just when it emerged from choas and outlined itself in my consciousness with startling distinctness. An event called it out of the mists and shadows into conscious reality. It happened on this wise:

There was a protracted meeting in our vicinity. A great and mysterious influence swept over the community. Many people, old and young, joined the church and were baptized. Doubtless in the beginning of the meeting the conversions were what I would now call genuine. Afterwards many merely went with the tide. To me it was only a curious spectacle. I had manifested no special interest except once or twice mechanically and experimenally. I had no conviction for sin. I had not felt lost and did not feel saved. First one and then another catechized me.

"Don't you believe the Bible? "Yes." "Don't you believe in Jesus Christ?" "Y-e-s." "Well, dosen't the Bible say that whoever believes in Jesus Christ is saved?" "Yes."

Now, mark three things: First, this catechizing was by zealous church-members. Second, the answers were historical as from a textbook. Third, I was only thirteen years old. They reported to the preachers: "Here is a lad who believes the Bible, believes in Jesus Christ and believes that he is saved. Ought not such a one to join the church?" Now came the pressure of well-meant but unwise persuasion. The whole thing would have been exposed, if when I presented myself for membership, I had been asked to tell my own story without prompting or leading questions. I did not have any to tell and would have told none. But many had joined, the hour was late, the die was cast.

Until after my baptism everything seemed unreal, but walking home from the baptism the revelation came. The vague infidelity of all the past took positive shape, and would not down at my bidding. My answers had been educational. I did not believe that the Bible was God's revelation. I did not believe in miracles or the divinity or vicarious sufferings of Jesus. I had no confidence in conversion and regeneration. There was no perceptible change in my disposition or affections. What I once loved, I still loved; what I once hated, I still hated. It was no temporary depression as sometimes comes to genuine Christians.

Joining the church, with its assumption of obligations acted on me like a touch of Ithuriel's spear. I saw my real self. I knew that either I had no religion or it was not worth having. The sensation of actual and positive infideliy was so new to me that I hardly knew what to say about it. I felt a repugnance to parade it. I wanted time and trial for its verification. I knew that its avowal would pain and horrify my family and the church, yet honesty required me to say something.

So I asked that the church withdraw from me on the ground that I was not converted. This was not granted because the brethren thought that I mistook temporary mental depression for lack of conversion. They asked me to give it a trial; to read the Bible and pray. From that time on I read the Bible as never before—read it all many times; studied it in the light of my infidelity; marked its contradictions and fallacies, as they seemed to me, from Genesis to Revelation. Two years passed. In this interval we moved to Texas. In a meeting when I was fifteen years old, I was persuaded to retain membership for further examination.

Now came the period of reading Christian apologies and infidel books. What a multitude of them of both kinds! Hume, Paine, Volney, Bolingbroke, Rousseau, Voltaire, Taylor, Gibbon, and others, over against Watson, Nelson, Horn, Calvin, Walker and a host of others. In the meantime I was at college devouring the Greek, Roman and Oriental philosophies. At seventeen, being worn out in body and mind, I joined McCullough's Texas Rangers, the first regiment mustered into the Confederate service, and on the remote, uninhabited frontier pursued the investigation with unabated ardor.

Then came another event. It came from no sin on my part, but it blasted every hope and left me in Egyptian darkness. The battle of life was lost. In seeking the field of war, I sought death. By peremptory demand I had my church connection dissolved and turned utterly away from every semblance of Bible belief to infidelity. This time I brought it a broken heart and a disappointed life, asking for light and peace and rest. It was no no curious speculation; no tentative intellectual examination. It was a stricken soul, anxiously and earnestly seeking light.

As I was in the first Confederate regiment, so I was in the last corps that surrendered; but while armies grappled and throttled each other, a darker and deadlier warfare raged within me. My quest for the truth was sincere and unintermittent. Happy people whose lives are not blasted may affect infidelity, may appear to its oracles from a curious, speculative interest, and may minister to their intellectual pride by seeming to be odd.

It was not so with me. With all the earnestness of a soul between which and happiness the bridges were burned, I brought a broken and bleeding, but honest heart to every reputed oracle of infidelity. I did not ask life, fame or pleasure. I merely asked light to shine on the path of right. Once more I viewed the anti-Christian philosophies, no longer to admire them in what they destroyed, but to inquire what they built up, and offered to a hungry heart and blasted life. There now came to me a revelation as awful as when Mokanna, in Moore's *Lalla Rookh* lifted his veil for Zelica.

Why had I never seen it before: These philosophies were mere negations; they overturned but built up nothing. I say nothing; I mean nothing. To the unstricken, curious soul, they are as beautiful as the aurora borealis, shining on arctic icebergs. But to me they warmed and melted nothing. No flowers bloomed and no fruit ripened under their cheerless beams. They looked down on my bleeding heart as the cold, distant, pitiless stars have ever looked down on all human suffering. Whoever, in his hour of real need, rests on abstract philosophy, makes cold, hard granite his pillow. Whoever looks trustingly into its false faces, looks into the face of Medusa, and is turned to stone. They are all wells without water, and clouds without rain in a parching drouth.

In the soul's hour of need who can conjure by the name of Voltaire? Of what avail is Epicurus or Zeno, Huxley or Darwin? Here was my case: I had turned my back on Christianity, and had found nothing in infidelity; happiness was gone and death would not come.

The Civil War had left me a wounded cripple on crutches, utterly poverty-stricken and loaded with debt. The internal war of infidelity, after making me roll hopelessly the ever-falling stone of Sisyphus, vainly climb the revolving wheel of Ixion, and stoop like Tantalus to drink waters that ever receded, or reach out for fruit that could not be grasped, now left me bound like Prometheus on the cold rock, while vultures tore with beak and talons a life that could suffer, but could not die.

At this time, two books of the Bible took hold of me with unearthly power. I knew from my experience that they were neither fiction or allegory—Job and Ecclesiastes. Some soul had walked those paths. They were histories, not dreams and not mere poems. Like Job, I believed in God; and like him had cried: "Oh, that I knew where I might find him', that I might come even to his seat! . . . Behold, I go forward but he is not there: and backward, but I cannot perceive him: on the left

hand, where he doth work, but I cannot behold him: he hideth
himself on the right hand, that I cannot see him: but he know-
eth the way that I take."

Like Job, I could not find answers in nature to the heart's
sorest need and the most important questions; and, like Job, regarding God as my adversary, I had cried out for a revelation:
"Oh, that one would hear me! behold, my desire is, that the
Almighty would answer me, and that mine adversary had written a book. Surely I would take it upon my shoulder, and bind
it as a crown to me." Like Job, I felt the need of a mediator,
who as a man could enter into my case, and as divine could enter
into God's case; and, like Job, I had complained: "He is not a
man as I am, that I should answer him, and we should come
together in judgment. Neither is there any daysman betwixt
us, that might lay his hand upon us both."

Thus I approached my twenty-second year. I had sworn
never to put my foot in another church. My father had died
believing me lost. My mother—when does a mother give up a
child?—came to me one day and begged, for her sake, that I
would attend one more meeting. It was a Methodist camp
meeting, held in the fall of 1865. I had not an atom of interest
in it. I liked the singing, but the preaching did not touch me.

But one day I shall never forget. It was Sunday at eleven
o'clock. The great, wooden shed was crowded. I stood on the
out-skirts, leaning on my crutches, wearily and somewhat scorn-
fully enduring. The preacher made a failure even for him. But
when he came down, as I supposed to exhort as usual, he start-
led me not only by not exhorting, but by asking some questions
that seemed meant for me.

He said: "You that stand aloof from Christianity and scorn
us simple folks, what have you got? Answer honestly before
God, have you found anything worth having?" My heart answered: "Nothing under the whole heaven; absolutely nothing."
As if he had heard my unspoken answer, he continued: "Is
there anything else out there with promise worth trying?" Again
my heart answered: "Nothing, absolutely nothing. I have been
to the jumping-off place on all these roads. They lead to a bot-
tomless abyss." "Well, then," he continued, "admitting there's
nothing there, if there be a God, mustn't there be a something

somewhere? If so, how do you know it is not here? Are you willing to test it? I don't ask you to read any book, nor study any evidences, nor make any pilgrimages. Are you willing to try it now; to make a practical, experimental test, you to be the judge of the result?"

These calm and pertinent questions hit me with tremendous force, but I didn't understand the test. He continued: "I base my test on these two Scriptures: 'If any man willeth to do his will, he shall know of the doctrine whether it be of God'; "Then shall we know if we follow on to know the Lord.' " For the first time I understood the import of these Scriptures. I had never before heard of such a translation. In our version it says "If any man will do the will of God, he shall know of the doctrine whether it be of God." But the preacher quoted it: "Whosoever willeth to do the will of God," showing that the knowledge as to whether the doctrine was of God depended not upon external action or exact conformity with God's will, but upon the internal disposition. In the second Scripture was also new light: "Then shall we know if we follow on to know the Lord," which means that true knowledge follows persistence in the prosecution of it.

So, when he invited all who were willing to make an immediate experimental test to come forward and give him their hands, I went forward. I was not prepared for the stir which this created. My infidelity and my hostile attitude toward Christianity were so well known in the community that such action developed quite a sensation. Some even began to shout. Whereupon, to prevent misconception, I arose and stated that I was not converted; that my heart was as cold as ice; my action meant no more than that I was willing to make an experimental test of the truth and power of the Christian religion, and to persist in subjection to the test until a true solution could be found. This quieted matters.

The meeting closed without any change upon my part. The last sermon had been preached, the benediction pronounced and the congregation was dispersing. A few ladies only remained, seated near the pulpit and singing. Feeling that the experiment was ended and the solution not found, I remained to hear them sing. As their last song they sang:

O land of rest, for thee I sigh,
   When will the moment come
When I shall lay my armor by
   And dwell in peace at home.

The singing made a wonderful impression upon me. Its tones were as soft as the rustling of angels' wings. Suddenly there flashed upon my mind, like a light from heaven, this Scripure: "Come unto me all ye that labour and are heavy laden, and I will give you rest." I did not see Jesus with my eye, but I seemed to see him standing before me, looking reproachfully and tenderly and pleadingly, seeming to rebuke me for having gone to all other sources for rest but the right one, and now inviting me to come to Him. In a moment I went, once and forever, casting myself unreservedly for all time at his feet, and in a moment the rest came, indescribable and unspeakable, and it has remained from that day until now.

I gave no public expression of the change which had passed over me, but spent the night in the enjoyment of it and wondering if it would be with me when morning came. When the morning came, it was still with me, brighter than the sunlight and sweeter than the songs of birds, and now for the first time, I understood the Scripture which I had often heard my mother repeat: "Ye shall go out with joy, and be led forth with peace: the mountains and the hills shall break forth before you into singing, and all the trees of the field shall clap their hands" (Isa. 55:12).

When I reached home, I said nothing, but the experience could not be hidden. As I was walking across the floor on my crutches, an orphan boy whom my mother had raised called attention to the fact that I was both whistling and crying. I knew that my mother heard him, and to avoid observation, went at once to my room, lay down on my bed and covered my face with my hands. I heard her coming. She pulled my hands away and gazed long and steadfastly without a word. A light came over her face as the shining on the face of Stephen; and with trembling lips, she said: "My son, you have found the Lord." Her happiness was indescribable. I don't think she slept that night. She seemed to fear that she might dream and wake to find that the glorious fact was but a vision of the night.

I spent the night at her bedside reading *Pilgrim's Progress.*
When I came with the pilgrims to the Beulah land, from which
Doubting Castle could be seen no more forever, and which was
within sight of the Heavenly City and within sound of the heavenly music, my soul was filled with a rapture and ecstacy of
joy such as I had never before experienced. I knew then as well
as I know now, that I would preach; that it would be my life
work; that I would have no other.

CHAPTER IV

W. T. CONNER

AUTOBIOGRAPHICAL SKETCH

I was born January 19, 1877, in Cleveland County, Arkansas, between Pine Bluff and Warren. My father owned a small farm. He was married twice, and had one boy by his first wife and six boys and two girls by his second. Four boys and one girl survive.

We lived at the place indicated until I was about thirteen and then moved to the western part of the same country near Kingsland, where my father worked at a saw mill, hauling logs and lumber. When I was nearly sixteen we moved eight miles west of Abilene, Texas. I have lived in Texas ever since then, except three years in seminaries.

My earliest religious impressions go back to the church where my parents and grandmother belonged in Cleveland County, Arkansas. These impressions were deepened in Kingsland community, but I was not converted until I reached Texas and attended an old-time, hurrah, Methodist meeting in the summer of 1894.

The man who baptized me was W. M. Reynolds. In the summer of 1895 J. M. Reynolds, his brother, held a meeting in our church. He asked me if I thought I was called to preach. I answered in the affirmative. He arranged with the pastor and church to license me and helped to get started by making appointments in the adjoining communities. I shall always be grateful for his assistance. My impression to preach, however, runs back to the time when I was a small boy, and became a definite conviction soon after I was converted.

Up to the time that I began to try to preach, I had never gone to any but ungraded country schools on an average of three of four months a year and some years practically none. In '95 or '96 I went to Simmons College (now Hardin-Simmons University) for about two or three months. I attended one full session in '96 and '97 and most of '97-'98.

In the fall of 1898 I entered Baylor, borrowing money from C. P. Warren, the father-in-law of Dr. L. R. Scarborough. Then I dropped out and taught school two years to pay back a debt of fifty dollars. In the winter of '98-'99 I taught at Anderson's Chapel in Jones County and the next winter at Lawn in the southern part of Taylor County. During the winter that I taught in Jones County, I preached for the church at Tuscola, Texas, my first pretense at being a pastor. The next winter while living at Lawn, I preached for my home church in Caps, in the community where I had been converted.

During my first year in Baylor, I came in contact with John S. Tanner, the most dynamic teacher I ever knew. I had a year with him in English Bible and also studied college algebra and solid geometry with him.

The fall of 1901 I went back to Baylor and stayed until January, 1903, and dropped out to help a brother go there. He was called to preach but died in 1910 having contracted tuberculosis while at Simmons. I preached at Eagle Lake half-time and quarter-time each at Rock Island and East Bernard. In the fall of 1904 I went back to Baylor and graduated with the A.B. degree in 1906. Two women at Eagle Lake, Mrs. F. O. Norris and her sister, Mrs. Green, sent me over a hundred dollars to help on expenses in Baylor. In those days a hundred dollars was a hundred dollars.

Among those who graduated in the class of 1906 was Miss Blanche Horne, who later taught Latin in the high school at Hillsboro. On June 4, 1907 we were married. Dr. S. P. Brooks asked me to teach Latin in Baylor the following year since Dr. Daniel, the professor of Latin, was ill. I accepted on condition that he would let my wife teach half of it. He readily agreed because he knew she was the better Latin teacher. I stayed at Baylor and studied in what was then the Baylor Theological Seminary taking the Th.B. and A.M. degrees in 1908.

That fall I went to Rochester and graduated in 1909—no degree being given then on graduation. I stayed on a graduate scholarship another year, wrote a thesis at the suggestion of Professor Walter Rauschenbusch on the "Theology of Theodore Parker", and received the B.D. degree. In the late spring of 1910 I went to the University of Chicago and studied about two weeks under Dr. George B. Foster. About the first or the middle of June I came back to Texas and was Associational Missionary in the Alvarado (now Johnson County) Association.

In the fall of 1910 I succeeded Dr. Calvin Goodspeed as teacher of Theology at Southwestern and have taught ever since. I have had two periods of study away. One was six weeks in the summer of 1920 at the University of Chicago. The other was during most of 1914 at the Southern Seminary. I had a major in Theology with Dr. E. Y. Mullins, a minor in the philosophy of Religion with Dr. W. O. Carver, and a minor in the Phychology of Religion with Dr. B. H. De Ment.

In the summer of 1920 I received a D.D. degree from Baylor. I have engaged in numerous activities, including lectures at summer assemblies. Altogether I have written twelve books, including *Christian Doctrine, Revelation and God, The Faith of the New Testament* and *The Gospel of Redemption.*

In our family we have five daughters and one son, all grown and still living. Their names are: Mary, John Davis, Arnette, Blanche Ray, Neppie Lee and Sarah Frances. All are married except Neppie Lee, who teaches art in the University of Arkansas. We have five granddaughters and three grandsons.

THE PLACE OF PRAYER IN THE CHRISTIAN LIFE

The place of prayer in the Christian life is a vital one. Sometimes people raise the question as to whether or not it is legitimate for one to pray for salvation. To my mind there is no question about that. The question would rather be whether one is a Christian if he has not prayed at least in spirit.

Salvation comes from God. It comes as a free gift and if one has not at least assumed the attitude of asking for God's mercy, there would be a serious question as to whether he could be a Christian. God gives and we receive. If we want to receive, then we should ask. I do not mean by this that one should necessarily speak words aloud or that he should repeat a certain formula, but I do mean that the spirit of looking to God, asking for mercy, and depending on him must be in our hearts if we are to receive his mercy and salvation.

As to the place of prayer in the Christian life, I should say that it is essential. Prayer is of the very essence of the Christian life. It is not something to be added on or left off, as an appendage to the Christian life, but something that belongs to the very essence and nature of that life. Communion with God is essential in being a Christian. With this general statement, I would like for us to consider several phases of this matter of prayer.

There are certain principles underlying prayer. One might call them presuppostions or fundamental principles in relation to prayer. Let it be understood that I am discussing this matter from the standpoint of the Christian revelation of God.

One of these principles is that we should believe in the reality of God. To pray is to assume that there is a Power above and beyond man on which man is dependent and from which Men's blessings come. One could hardly pray if he did not believe that there was such a Power. The Book of Hebrews tells us that one must believe that God is and that he is a rewarder of those that seek him. Here we are saying that underlying prayer is the implicit belief that such a Power exists and that man is related to that Power.

Moreover, prayer assumes that man is dependent. One of the deepest things in man's consciousness is the feeling of dependence. This feeling of dependence is so deeply embedded in man's consciousness that the German theologian Schleiermacher said that this sense of dependence was the essence of religion. He thus made religion universal. We might not care to make this the essence of religion with Schleiermacher, but we certainly could agree that this sense of dependence is deeply embedded in man's consciousness and is one of the reasons that prayer in some form is found among practically all peoples.

Another assumption underlying prayer is that God is personal. By this we are not to understand that God has the limitations of man. He is personal in the sense that he is intelligent and purposeful. He is not only intelligent, but he is the source of all intelligence in the universe. All the rational creatures of our universe have their being rooted in God. He is the source of all intelligence in life.

He is not purposeful in the sense that he has to question and debate and painfully work out his plans, but he is purposeful in the sense that he knows what he is about and moves toward the attainment of his fundamental intentions in relation to man and the world. He is personal in the sense that all finite personalities have the ground of their being in him and find their ultimate end in God. Some people have tried to maintain religion and even prayer in some form apart from belief in a personal God. But to say the least of it, prayer in the Christian sense without belief in the personality of God is impossible. What would thanksgiving or petition mean if there were no One to thank or no One from which we should ask.

Prayer also assumes that in some sense God is interested in man and in his welfare. The purpose of prayer is not to get God interested in man but to help in realizing the good will that God has toward man. One of the fundamental things in the Christians religion is God's love toward man. This love of God for man is expressed in the Greek New Testament by a word that means rational good will. Only once or twice do we find the verb used with reference to God's attitude toward man that denotes personal or intimate affection. Once or twice in the Gospel according to John such a word is used with reference to God's attitude toward the personal disciples of Jesus. In other places it is a word that means rational and purposeful good will. The New Testament gives us the impression that God from all eternity has had such good will toward man. In fact, in the First Epistle of John, we are told that God is love and the word used for love denotes this kind of good will.

So when we say that underlying prayer is the assumption that God has such good will toward man we are expressing what is implied in different ways in the New Testament with reference to this matter. Such an assumption does not necessarily belong to the general religious consciousness of mankind. It is an assumption involved in the Christian revelation of God.

The Christian assumption with reference to this matter is that God has a plan for our lives. Most any Christian whether he is Calvinistic or otherwise in his theology feels that somehow God has a plan for the life of each of his children and that prayer will help us to find and follow that plan. We are not to think of this plan as a dogmatic and arbitrary decree that interferes with our freedom or responsibilities with reference to our lives. Christians generally, however, do feel that by prayer and fellowship with God they can come into harmony with his will and find the direction in which he would have them go.

This is the direct contrary of what some people might think with reference to prayer. They might think of prayer as an effort on man's part to impose his plan and his will on God. People who misunderstand the nature and purpose of prayer have sometimes so spoken of it. They have denied the efficacy of prayer because they assumed that prayer was an effort to impose man's petty ideas and plans on God and bring God into line with these plans of man. The nature of prayer is just the opposite. It is not the purpose of prayer to bring God into line with man's ideas and purposes, but to bring man into harmony with God's plan and purpose for the one who prays.

Sometimes this question is raised with reference to prayer: If God is all-wise and good, if he knows what is best for us and wants to give us what is best, then why should we pray? Why not just leave God to give us what he knows to be best without trying to change or influence him in the matter?

Let me come back to emphasize that the teaching of Jesus is that God does know best. Jesus distinctly says that our

Father knows what we have need of before we ask him. Prayer, therefore, cannot be for the purpose of informing God. If we had to inform the Lord, we would in all likelihood misinform him. We would likely not give him true knowledge of the situation. If he were dependent on man's puny wisdom, he could not understand the true situation. He knows infinitely better what we need than we do. He looks ahead. He sees everything about us in true relation. He understands with a wisdom that is far above man.

Why, then, should we pray if God knows best what we need? Well, for one thing, Jesus wants us to come in our ignorance and blindness submitting ourselves to the infinite wisdom of God and trusting him to do what is best. We are to be enlightened by his wisdom, not that he is to be enlightened by ours.

Nor is the primary purpose of prayer to impose our wills on God. It is rather to bring us into line with his will and his purpose for us and our world. Jesus taught us to pray: "Thy kingdom come, thy will be done on earth as it is in heaven." The coming of his Kingdom means the reign of God in the hearts and lives of men. We are to pray for his will to be done in us and in the world in which we live.

Nor does this mean that we simply are to be passive in our attitude in regard to the matter. Our wills are to be active. We are to pray with energetic willing toward God and his work in the world. But while we are to be active and energetic, we are always to seek to bring our wills in line with his purposes and pray that our wills shall be done only as they are in line with his. We are to will in prayer but to will in harmony with the purposes of God and not contrary to his will I remember reading a statement from S. D. Gordon many years ago to this effect: that in prayer we do not work against God: we work *with* God. We are to pray as God's Spirit energizes in our hearts and brings us to will in harmony with him and his plan for us and the world. Jesus himself prayed: "Not my will, but thine be done" when such a prayer meant for agony and death. Such should be the Christian's attitude in prayer.

Let us come back to the question then: Since God knows and wills for us the best, why should we pray? We should pray on the ground that God in accomplishing his will in the world wants to take us into fellowship with him in bringing his purposes and plans. Prayer is the most personal act that a Christian ever performs in the religious life. It is the recognition of God as a Person of infinite knowledge and good will toward us and all mankind. It is our personal adjustment to him as such a Person. It is our effort to come into harmony with him as such a Person and try to help him work out his purposes and plans in our lives and the world.

We may not see all that God has in mind for us in willing that we should pray, but I think we can at least see this: Prayer is God's plan to take us up into fellowship with him in carrying out his purposes in the world. It might be put like this: In doing Christian work we do not simply find a general plan that God has laid down and seek to follow that plan by the use of our natural intelligence. God has, no doubt, such a general plan for each of us, but prayer makes God's plan for us intimate and personal. In prayer we seek to have such fellowship with God that we can work in intimate fellowship with him in carrying out his purposes in the world.

Take the matter of redemption which is central in the gospel of Christ. God's purpose for man is redemptive. He wants to take each of the sons of God into fellowship with himself in carrying out the purpose of redemption in relation to mankind. So when we ourselves experience redemption, he puts something of his own passion in our hearts for the salvation of others. In line with his purpose he prompts us by his Spirit to pray for others that they may be redeemed. He moves us to pray for those who are working as evangelists, missionaries, and in other forms of Christian service, for the redemption of men. In doing this, God takes us up into fellowship with himself and thereby transforms us more and more into his own image. The Spirit of Christ comes increasingly to possess us, move us, and control us in all our relations in life.

This means that to look on prayer simply as a means of getting "things" from God is to see prayer in a rather superficial light. I have read of prayer as a means of getting "things" from God. I do not mean to say that God does not sometimes give us things in answer to prayer, but I would say with emphasis that that is not the main purpose of prayer. The main purpose of prayer is to bring God himself into our lives and let God work out his purposes and plans in and through us. God himself is the answer to prayer. Prayer is not simply petition. It is much more than that. It includes adoration, thanksgiving, confession, intercession.   In all of this, we are coming into fellowship with God and God himself is coming into our lives. As God comes into our lives, he transforms us more and more into the image of the living and redeeming Christ.

One reason, then, why God wants us to pray is for our own sakes. It brings us closer to himself. It makes us more like himself. He is thereby carrying out his purpose of good will concerning us.

Do not understand by this, however, what has sometimes been called the reflex influence of prayer. A man like Immanuel Kant, the great philosopher, says plainly in his lectures on ethics that the reflex influence of prayer is the only benefit. He means by this evidently that there is no direct communion or personal touch of the spirit of man with the Spirit of God. Prayer only helps man, so he evidently thinks, because it enables man to bring himself into a better state of mind and heart.   Prayer would be only a man's effort to lift himself over the fence by his own bootstraps. I have not seen anybody able to get very high off the ground by such an effort. What I mean to say is that one reason God ordains for us to pray is because prayer brings us in fellowship with God and makes us like God. God himself is the answer to prayer.

I do not mean, however, that the blessing to the man who prays is the only benefit that comes from prayer. In ways that we do not understand God works his purposes in the lives of others in answer to our prayer. God energizes in the lives of others as we pray for them. One of the constant pleas of the apostle Paul was that his fellow Christians pray for him. He uses language that shows that he means that they agonize in prayer, that they thall labor in prayer. We can help other Christians around the world by praying for them. We can help men into the Kingdom of God by interceding for them.

I should like to emphasize also that there is what one might call a listening side to prayer. Some people consider one a good conversationalist if he will do all the listening and let them do all the talking. Some of us are like that in relation to God. We want God to listen and we want to do all the talking. In prayer we should listen for God's voice as he speaks to us. In fellowship with God in prayer there is light to be obtained on the problems and difficulties of life that can not be obtained any other way. If one wishes light from the face of God to illumine his way, he should listen attentively when he seeks to have fellowship with God.

Nor should we think of seeking God in prayer simply for our sakes. It is true that if we seek God and his will, abundant blessings will come to us. God is our chief need. In a true sense, God is our only need. But we have not yet been brought to the true view of the matter until we see that we should seek God for his own sake. We should adore and worship him because he is worthy of our adoration and worship. We should **make God the end** of prayer and worship, not man. If we seek God because of what he will do for us, we have not yet risen above the human plane. We should worship him for what he is within himself, not merely because of what he gives us. A good father or mother does not wish to be loved by a son or daughter for what the son or daughter thinks to get from loving the parent. True love is bestowed for the sake of the one loved, not for the sake of the lover.

One other word. How can one know about the reality and blessing of prayer? He can know in only one way, namely, by trying it. He cannot know by arguing. He cannot know merely by hearing about it. He cannot know even by reading the Bible. These things may give him suggestions, but he will really know for himself only as he tries it. Dr. S. P. Brooks told once about an incident that took place while he was a student in Baylor University. Brooks was a Christian. He had a friend who was not. This friend came to him one day and, calling him by his first name, said: "Palmer, do you suppose God would hear a man like me pray?" Those who knew Dr. Brooks will recognize his answer as characteristic of the man. He said: "The way to find out is to try." They went into the old tabernacle that used to stand back of where the First Baptist Church of Waco now stands. They got down on their knees and Brooks prayed, then the other man prayed, and God saved him. The way you find out about prayer is to try it out. There is no other way.

CHAPTER V

B. A. COPASS

AUTOBIOGRAPHICAL SKETCH

My ancestors came from Normandy to England in 1166. I have a book called *Brother Copass* written in England a century or so ago. The descendants of those who came with William have scattered over the countries wherever the English people have gone. My son, who was in World War II, found people by our name in New Zealand and Australia. My daughter found a number in the telephone directory in Vancouver, British Columbia. So gradually they drifted to the United States and to the South.

I was born in Clementsville, Tennessee, May 29, 1865. My parents were Charles Wesley and Lucinda (Bowman) Copass. Father's given name would suggest the vigorous Methodist heritage he had. I started life at the close of the Civil War when times were hard. Tennessee had seceded from the Union, was at the northern border of the Confederacy, and practically every square mile of land was fought over by the contending armies and the country largely laid waste. So I know from experience what it means to live under pinched conditions.

My early schooling was rather meager as educational facilities were very poor in our community in those difficult times. Our country schools were from three to five months in length. There were some years when they did not even open the schools due to financial difficulties. They were one-teacher schools with all classes reciting in the same room and we recited aloud while the others tried to carry on their studies. After some years in these irregular country schools I attended Willette Academy, a school founded and maintained for many years by the Baptists in those Tennessee hills.

We moved from Tennessee to Kentucky and much of my

early life was spent in that state. I attended Bethel College
at Russelville, Kentucky, receiving the A.B. degree in 1890 and
the A.M. in 1893. In 1898 the college conferred on me the D.D.
degree. I attended the Southern Baptist Theological Seminary
for three years (1891-1894) finishing the regular course of
studies which later became the Th.M. course. In those days
they did not give a degree, such not being considered as necessary to success as it is now. In the summer of 1919 I attended
the University of Chicago.

I was ordained to the ministry July 20, 1889. My first
pastorate was at Clinton, Kentucky (1894-96), where Clinton
College was located. Some of the students there in those days
became leaders later in different parts of the United States,
such as Dr. E. B. Atwood, Professor of Bible, in Hardin-
Simmons University. Other pastorates were at Los Angeles,
California (1896-98); Marksbury, Kentucky (1898-1901;
Waxahachie, Texas (1901-06); San Marcos, Texas (1906-12)
and Denton, Texas (1912-13). The longest pastorate was at
San Marcos where San Marcos Baptist Academy is located.
Through the church there I had much to do in establishing and
building the Academy. Two state schools are located at Den-
ton, and I enjoyed contact with students at these places.

For four years (1914-18) I served as Associate Secretary
of the State Board of Missions of the General Convention of
Texas. During that time I had the privilege of being associated
with Dr. J. B. Gambrell who was State Missions Secretary.
It was the opportunity of a life time. He was a remarkable
character and a counselor of rare ability. The experiences
connected with this work throughout Texas, together with the
pastorates held in various states, gave a fine background for
teaching preachers in Southwestern Seminary as head of the
Department of Old Testament Interpretation from 1918-1942.
I had previously declined a similar position in another seminary.

On May 29, 1894 (my birthday anniversary) I was married
to Miss Cloantha Williams, daughter of the vice-president of
Bethel College. She died in 1902. Of the four children born to
this union, three survive—Mrs. J. B. Kennedy, Jackson, Mississippi; Ben A., Iraan, Texas; and Mrs. A. J. Holgrean, Olympia,
Washington. I was married to Miss Crickett Keys of Waxa-

hachie, Texas, September 12, 1904. To this union three children were born, only one of whom, Lieut. Col. Mike Copass of Seattle, Washington, survives. My family has followed the Copass tradition of scattering to different parts of the country, only one being in Texas.

I am a Mason, a Democrat, a member of the Phi Gamma Delta Fraternity and the Texas Baptist Historical Society. My greatest pride and joy, however, have been in membership in a Baptist Church, for the hope of the world lies more in this institution than in all of the societies and fraternal organizations in existence. I have taken an active part in the prohibition movement and other activities for moral and social reform, as well as in the general work of the denomination.

Besides various articles written through the years for newspapers and magazines, I am the author of the following books: *The Message of Hosea* (1906), *A Manuel of Old Testament Theology* (1925), *Theology in Hebrew Words* (1934), *One God* (1935), *Amos* (1938), and *Isaiah, the Prince of Old Testament Prophets* (1943). I have done considerable lecturing at Bible institutes and assemblies.

I retired from teaching in 1942 and am now resting at my home near the Seminary, and doing the things which my physical strength permits. I have always tried to be faithful to every task imposed. Seminary Hill will continue to be the center of things for me until God calls me to go to Him.

PERFECT SALVATION*

"But of him are ye in Christ Jesus, who was made unto us wisdom from God, even righteousness and sanctification and redemption." I Cor. 1:30.

The merest glance at the text, shows two things, plainly evident: Salvation is all of God, and salvation is all through Jesus Christ. And the Christ preached by the Apostle, is the Christ of the Cross—"But we preach Christ crucified." "For I determined not to know anything among you save Jesus Christ, and Him crucified." The Christ of the resurrection was the Christ of the Cross. It was as if the Apostle was saying: "All the power that dwells in God to draw men out of sin, to holiness and to himself was actually in the cross."

And this general statement of the Apostle is all the more human and interesting, when we remember that the writer was dealing with a concrete and present situation. He had to deal there at Corinth with the two demands that always develop when human hearts come to deal with the question of religion. The demand for external manifestation of power, to prove the so-called religious message to be from God; and the demand for "wisdom," that will appeal to the speculative pride of the minds of men. "Jews ask for signs"— i.e., external manifestations of power; "Greeks seek after wisdom"—i.e., philosophic speculation concerning God, the universe and men.

In the presence of these organized demands the great apostle held up Jesus Christ—"Christ the power of God and the wisdom of God."

As the City of Corinth and the Church in Corinth were more largely Greek than Jew, emphasis is laid upon Christ as wisdom from God. Such is true in our text: "Who was made unto us wisdom from God." This indeed is the message of the text. The remaining portion of the text is but an explanation of "Christ Jesus—wisdom from God"—even righteousness and sanctification and redemption."

I. Righteousness

Christ Jesus, as wisdom from God, becomes to men and for

*Texas State Baptist Convention Sermon, preached at Fort Worth, Nov. 7, 1912.

men righteousness. This one word raises by implication the whole question of man's sinfulness and his resultant separation from a holy God. It implies that, if man returns to God, he must have righteousness, and a righteousness, that he himself cannot acquire. Another must provide it for him. This, God himself did when He provided Christ Jesus, "Him who knew no sin, He (God) made to be sin on our behalf, that we might become the righteousness of God in Him."

This word of our text makes no reference to any change in the character of one who comes to God through Christ, but rather to His standing before God in Christ. God sees not man's sinfulness, but his own righteousness as manifested and applied in Jesus.

This manifestation and application of righteousness through Christ, makes possible and actual man's justification in the sight of God. As some one explains: "That judicial act of God, by which, on account of Christ to whom the sinner is united by faith, he declares that sinner to be no longer exposed to the penally of law, but to be restored to his favor. The reversal of God's attitude toward the sinner, because of the sinner's new relation to Christ. God did condemn, He now acquits."

A Greek once stood before a tribunal charged and proved guilty of treason against his country. The judge asked whether any one knew a reason why the prisoner should not be sentenced and ordered to execution. At this juncture a man stepped forth from the spectators and held up two stumps of arms. He said: "I gave my two hands in behalf of my country in honorable battle. The man is guilty, but he is my brother. I plead these two stumps of arms in behalf of my brother." That plea set his brother free. Even so, the Christ of the cross, the wisdom from God, the righteousness of God takes sinful man's place before God, and man goes free. Not because he actually is righteous, but because God in Christ is righteousness.

Anselm, Archbishop of Canterbury about 1100 A.D. wrote a tract called "Consolations for the Dying." In that tract he stated in a concise and striking way the truth of the thought before us. In the form of dialogue he put it: "Dost thou believe that the Lord Jesus died for thee? I believe it. Dost thou thank Him for His passion and death? I do thank Him. Dost thou believe that thou canst not be saved except by His death? I believe it. Come then while life remainest in thee; in His death alone place thy whole trust, in naught else place thy trust; to His death commit thyself wholly; with this alone cover thyself wholly. And if the Lord thy God will to judge thee, say: 'Lord, between thee and me, I present the death of our Lord Jesus Christ, not otherwise can I content with thee.' And if He shall say that thou art a sinner, say thou: 'Lord, I interpose the death of our Lord Jesus Christ between my sins and thee.' If He says that thou hast deserved condemnation, say: 'Lord, I set the death of our Lord Jesus Christ between my evil deserts and thee; and His merits I offer for those which I ought to have and have not.' If He shall say that He is wrath with thee, say: 'Lord, I oppose the death of our Lord Jesus Christ between thy wrath and me.' And when thou hast completed this, say again: 'Lord, I set the death of our Lord Jesus Christ between thee and me.' "

This glorious plea is made possible because "Christ Jesus is made unto us wisdom from God, even righteousness." Without this work of Christ in behalf of the sinner, justification before God would be utterly and forever impossible. Here is the dividing line between despair and hope; darkness and light; destruction and salvation.

II. Sanctification

Christ Jesus as wisdom from God becomes to the justified person, sanctification. Some people are much afraid of that word because certain other people have made extravagant, foolish, even sinful claims concerning it. But this good word is found throughout the Bible, from the first book to the last; and holds within its meaning a vital Bible doctrine. It teaches that salvation even for this life, is only begun at the moment of justification. When the soul accepts Christ by faith as a personal Saviour, the Divine life is implanted in that soul by the Holy Spirit. The Spirit who gave that life to the soul abides with it, nurtures it, trains it, develops it, until, in actual character, it is like unto Jesus Christ. In every warfare, struggle, heart longing and aspiration after God and holiness the spirit of God in Christ is present to strengthen, guide and give victory.

Thus we understand that "The work of Jesus (in behalf of the sinner) for this life is two-fold. It is a work accomplished for us, destined to effect reconciliation between God and man: it is a work accomplished in us, with the object of effecting our sanctification. By the one, a right relation is established between God and us; by the other, the fruit of the re-established order is secured. By the former the condemned sinner is received into a state of grace; by the latter the pardoned sinner is associated with the life of God." Justification is the photographer making the negative; sanctification is the photographer developing the negative into the finished picture. Justifictation is the woman placing leaven in the measure of meal; sanctification is the process whereby the whole becomes leavened.

In the latter portion of Rom. 7 the Apostle shows the hopelessness of the struggle for holiness, if the battle is fought alone. The most that can be accomplished is the cry: "Wretched man that I am! Who shall deliver me out of the body of this death?" But in chapter 8 a new personality enters the struggle. That personality is the Spirit of God; and in Him victory is assured. "There is therefore now no condemnation to them that are in Christ Jesus. For the law of the Spirit of Life in Christ Jesus has made me free from the law of sin and death." The saved man is under the law of the Spirit of life. He is therefore, free from the law of sin and death under which he once lived. The outworking and completion of that law of the Spirit must come. That completion is the fulness of the Christ life; or Christ-likeness in character.

We then, as Christians having this hope, are not to allow sin to reign in our mortal bodies. Sin is still there, and will be there so long as we are in this body of our humiliation, but it must be put under foot in the life and power of the Spirit. A struggle there will be, sharp and constant, but victory is sure.

A petulant woman once said to this speaker: "If I ever do become a Christian, I am going to be a good one." The speaker replied: "From the way you have been talking you will be a very poor one. You will spend life battling with your temper." Wide eyed she asked: "What then, is the use of religion?" To which we replied: "To insure us final victory over sin in the Holy Spirit. As you are, you are doomed to defeat here and hereafter. Your struggle is useless without Christ." And, friends, we are permitted to see those who have fought that battle long and arduously, and have almost won. There is almost a halo about their faces as their life's sun is setting.

This preacher was once sent for by an old man who was nearing the end of life's journey. He had a trust to commit to the younger man. As I entered his room he said: "I cannot talk much. First, kneel by my bedside and pray that God's will, in my case, may be done." After the prayer he said: "Now bend over me. Lift my arms about your neck and let me kiss your face. As I near the portal, God gives it to me to love my brethren better." As I looked into that old face, it seemed that I could see a little of the glory. His battle was almost won. His victory was almost complete. In a few days he saw face to face Him who was his sanctification.

III. Redemption

Christ Jesus as wisdom from God becomes to the justified, sanctified person redemption. In its full and complete significence redemption includes and covers all that has been said and more. It lies back of justification and sanctification, and makes both possible. But the Scriptures lay emphasis upon two points of application. An illustration of the first is found in Eph. 1:7 "In whom we have our redemption through His blood even the forgiveness of our trespasses according to the riches of His grace." The meaning here is too obvious to need discussion. But emphasis is also laid upon another point of application. An instance is found in Rom. 8:22-23, "For we know, that the whole creation groaneth and travaileth together in pain until now, and not only so, but ourselves also, who have the first fruits of the spirit, even we ourselves groan within ourselves, waiting for our adoption to-wit: The redemption of our body."

This latter is the sense in which the word is used in our text. The Apostle was looking to that final victory and deliverance from even the presence of sin; when the body too will be redeemed and made like unto the body of the glory of Jesus Christ.

Salvation is more than something past. "Salvation is something past, something present and something future. A past fact, justification; a present process, sanctification; a future

consumation, redemption and glory." If the past fact has been
accomplished within a soul, the present and the future are assured. "For our citizenship is in heaven; whence also we wait
for a Savior, the Lord Jesus Christ; who shall fashion anew the
body of our humiliation, that it may be conformed unto the body
of His glory, according to the working whereby He is able even
to subject all things unto Himself." These bodies of ours are
now full of sin, pain and death. They will go to the grave and
corruption, if our Lord delay His coming. But when He comes
these bodies will be raised from the dead, and fashioned anew
like unto the glorified body of Jesus Christ. We will be like
Him, spirit and body and the salvation already begun and now
in process will be complete.

This blessed hope is not only for the Christian personally,
but it comforts in the tenderest and most sacred relations of
life. Many persons in this audience know something of the sorrows and bereavements of the speaker since he has been in
Texas, now eleven years. Four times has he seen the bodies
of loved ones go to the grave. One of those deaths was so full
of glory that he may be permitted to describe it. A little boy,
his father's constant companion, was going. The little fellow
was motherless. Just before he left he said: "Father, take me
into your arms." After a few moments he said: "Put me into
the bed again." He seemed to know that his father held his
body on earth for the last time. Then he said: "I want father
and auntie and Cloantha and Benjamin and Clarissa (the members of the family including the servant girl) to go with me."
In a few moments his spirit went away and we carried the little
body to the grave on the morrow. But, beloved, I shall see him
again in the body. His body, no longer subject to pain and
death, but glorified. Then we will part never again, but be
together with Jesus who is our redemption.

We need to see the Christ as the center and sum of all
things pertaining to the relation of God and men.

"What the hand is to the lute,
What the breath is to the flute,
What is fragrance to the smell;
What the spring is to the dell,
What the flower is to the bee,

That is Jesus Christ to me.

What the mother to the child,
What the Guide in pathless wild,
What is oil to troubled wave,
What is ransom to the slave,
What is water to the sea,
That is Jesus Christ to me.

And with this Saviour as our Saviour now and forever, and
this message of Christ Jesus as wisdom from God even righteousness and sanctification and redemption, and in this power
of the Holy Spirit, we are to go to a lost world and preach
the Christ of the Cross as did the great Apostle at Ephesus and
Corinth. We need no new message for the Twentieth Century, but the old story of abounding grace and redeeming love.
We need to preach perfect and eternal salvation in the cross
of Calvary.

"Exalt the cross! its awful shape
   Athwart the blood red sky,
Shall turn the nations of the earth
      To Him of Calvary.

Exalt the cross! its outstretched arms,
   To all the world proclaim
The passion of a Savior's love,
   The glory of his name.

Beyond all human ken,
   Exalt the cross! its mystery,
Shall break the hearts, wash white the souls
   Of multitudes of men.

Exalt the cross! its feebleness,
   Transfigured Divine,
Shall shake the whole great teeming earth,
   Christ conquers in this sign."

Chapter VI

J. W. CROWDER

AUTOBIOGRAPHICAL SKETCH

I was born of American parents on a farm near Hayesville, Tennessee, March 27, 1873. I lived and worked on this farm with the family of nine children until I was grown.

My family was poor and educational advantages were meager. My first school was the "Old Field School" three and one-half miles away. To this school I walked with my oldest brother when I was six years old. My first book was Webster's *Blue Back Speller*. After two years we were transferred to the Hayesville school, where we had college men for our teachers, one of whom especially inspired me with visions of the possibilities for a country boy.

Inspired thus, and stimulated by the examples of Abraham Lincoln and James A. Garfield, I split rails and did all kinds of farm work. Like Lincoln, I studied by the light of the fireplace, and like Garfield, the tow-boy, carried my books with me to my daily tasks. Having gone as far as possible in my studies with the constant calls from the farm, I bought my freedom from my father for three months, by which I was able to prepare for teaching in Tennessee. Then I entered High School at Lafayette, ten miles from home, and walked back for the week-ends in order to make my limited funds hold out.

I organized my first school at Hayesville, Tennessee, January 3, 1893. This was the beginning of a public service of fifty years—two in Tennessee, three in Kentucky, and forty-five in Texas.

In 1897 I came to Texas and taught in the public schools four years, during which time I entered the ministry. I was "liberated", or licensed, by the Weston Baptist Church, September 30, 1899; preached my first sermon October 6; was called to the pastorate of the Honey Creek Baptist Church, January 20, 1900; and was ordained March 3 of the same year. During more than forty years of ministry, I have held fourteen pastorates in Texas: six in Collin County, two in Hill, one in Freestone, one in Robertson, one in Ellis, two in Fort Worth, and one in Parker County.

I was married in Tennessee to Miss Allie May Morrow, June 1, 1897. To this union were born two children, Carroll and Noma, both of whom survive. On April 1, 1934, my first wife passed away. On May 11, 1935, I was married to Mrs. May Fair of Sherman, Texas, a registered nurse and welfare worker. We have lived on Seminary Hill twelve years.

In October, 1905, I moved from Celina to Waco for study in Baylor University, enrolling for an A.B. degree, including Latin and Greek. At the same time I became a student with Dr. B. H. Carroll and after four years of study received from his hand in 1908 the special degree of the English Bible (E.B.). In 1909 Dr. Carroll asked me to become his assistant in the English Bible Department of the Seminary, looking to becoming his successor as teacher. At first I declined intending to go to Yale after finishing in Baylor, but in response to his urgent request I reconsidered and decided to go with him. This Dr. W. W. Lackey has admirably expressed in verse thus:

"Eschewing fame and bright career,
He chose to walk with the greatest seer."

In 1910 I came with the Seminary to Fort Worth and finished my course in absentia in Baylor, receiving the Classical A.B. degree in 1911. In the meantime I was carrying forward my work on the Th.M. degree in the Seminary. This course was pursued until work in the following departments was finished: Church History, Homiletics, Systematic Theology, Missions, New Testament Greek, Hebrew and English Bible. In addition I did by correspondence one year each in Temple University, the University of Chicago, and Webster University for which the D.D. degree was received in 1934.

All my teaching in Tennessee, Kentucky and Texas was done under first grade certificates. During the four years with B. H. Carroll I made an average of 98 plus on the whole Bible and in Senior Greek, an average of 99½. My record in Baylor

University was summed up in the college annual, "Baylor Round-Up", for 1911 with the encomium, "He was a scholar, and a ripe and good one."

In 1901 Dr. Carroll appointed me custodian of his lectures on the English Bible, and, later, compiler and reviser of his manuscripts. Of the thirty-five volumes published, I have furnished the manuscripts for all except four, and now have the manuscripts for fifteen more, which I am editing for publication. Also have published the book: *Dr. B. H. Carroll the Colossus of Baptist History.*

At Dr. Carroll's death in 1914 I became Professor of English Bible in the Southwestern Baptist Theological Seminary and taught in this capacity for five years. Then I became director of the Seminary Extension Department, in which I labored twenty-four years. In the meantime I was made director of the Seminary's floral interests and labored in that field fifteen years, teaching Introductory Greek during this time.

On June 1, 1943, I retired from active service with the Seminary to finish the task assigned by Dr. Carroll. At this time the faculty of the Seminary in presenting publicly a gift expressed their approval of my service with emphasis on two words: "Faithful and Efficient."

OPPORTUNITY*

Text: "So then, as we have opportunity, let us work that which is good toward all men." Galatians 6:10.

Whatever Paul may have been discussing as a subject here, he enlarges in this text so as to include the great purpose of our lives—to do good toward all men. The rest of the sentence reads: "and especially toward them that are of the household of the faith." It is not this limited phase of the text, however, that we wish to consider this evening, but the broader phase which sets forth our duty "toward all men."

I offer as preliminary to this discourse two equations for your consideration, viz.:

1. Gifts and training equal ability.
2. Ability and opportunity equal responsibility.

By combining these two equations and then subtracting "ability" from both members, we have this equation:

Gifts and training and opportunity equal responsibility.

In this equation we see that opportunity has two antecedents—gifts and training. These terms stand in the order of their relations. Now let us give some attention to these antecedents.

What do we mean by gifts? Our gifts are the potentialities within us, whether latent or developed. These, whether developed, constitute the sum total of our power to do. They are of God. Paul said of Christ, "When he ascended on high he led captivity captive and gave gifts unto men." No one is responsible for a lack of them, but the responsibility rests upon him who has the gift.

Next, in order, is training. By this we mean education, that which develops the latent powers within us. That is the best training which recognizes God at every point, hence, Christian education is the best education. One may have great gifts and yet not have great ability, due to the lack of training. Effective training requires much study and diligent practice. Nor would we lose sight of the great fact that God not only

*Sermon preached before the Collin County Baptist Association at Melissa, Texas, September 8, 1903, and published in the *Baptist Standard* by request of the congregation.

gives gifts, but He gives opportunity for the development of them. At this point our responsibility begins.

Now let us consider

I. The source and nature of opportunity.

"As we have opportunity." The word here translated "opportunity" means "a fit or favorable time." Since this word enters very largely into our responsibility, we wish to note

1. Opportunities are God-given. We certainly are not living in a world of chance. All we have and are is of God, and therefore the glory belongs to Him. This is strikingly illustrated in the case of Joseph, who was sold into Egyptian slavery. It was a dark hour for him when his brothers exchanged him for twenty pieces of silver, and darker when belied and cast into prison. Then he interprets two dreams and is forgotten. After two full years the king dreams, and Joseph interprets his dreams by the power of God, for which he is promoted to second place in the kingdom. Did it come by chance? Nay; verily, "God was with him and prospered him."

We see the Son of God as He sat by the well at Sychar, wearied with His journey, while the disciples have gone into the city to buy food. A strange thing occurred—a woman came to draw water at noon, it being the custom to come in the early morning or late afternoon. Did it just happen? Nay; when we see the glorious results we understand that God was just giving His beloved Son opportunity.

When Paul saw the man of Macedonia and heard him calling for help, he understood that God was giving him opportunity to preach the Gospel unto the Macedonians. It has been said that we make our own opportunities, but in a very limited sense is this true—only in the sense of one opportunity being a stepping-stone to another.

2. Opportunities are successive. They do not all come at once, but only one at a time. Our great concern should be the present opportunity. Those of the past are gone forever; those of the future are yet to come. So, then, our concern should be for the thing in hand. They are successive, also, in the fact that one may be the door to another. The opportunity of today is so often the door to the one of tomorrow.

3. Opportunities for service were never more numerous than

they are today. If I were to name this age, I would call it
the Age of Opportunity. Why the railroads? To send the
Gospel to every nook and corner of the nation. Why the
great steamers? To carry the missionaries to foreign lands.
All the discoveries and inventions mean nothing less than opportunity.

Gray, in his "Elegy in a Country Churchyard," paid fine
tribute to the capabilities of our less fortunate ancestors in the
following stanza:

"Full many a gem of purest ray serene,
The dark unfathomed caves of ocean bear;
Full many a flower is born to blush unseen
And waste its sweetness on the desert air."

No poet will have the right to sing thus over our graves.
If we close our eyes to the opportunities God has given us, let
their song be the dirge of lost opportunities. The missionary
opportunity is far greater now than ever before in the history of
the world. God has opened the last door, and now missionaries
may enter every nation under the canopy of heaven.

4. The value of an opportunity is measured by the value of
the thing involved in the opportunity. One who neglects an
opportunity to rescue a perishing child is regarded as a criminal,
because of the value put upon human life. How much more
should one be regarded a criminal who neglects an opportunity
to rescue a perishing soul. Whoever has been instrumental in
God's hand in leading a soul to Christ is far richer than one
who has gained the whole world.

5. We must look for opportunities. We are not likely to
enter an open door if we do not see it. After our Lord had
revealed Himself to the Samaritan woman at the well of Sychar
as the Messiah, and she had sped the good news into the city,
the people came forth in multitudes to see the Prophet. Then
He turned to His disciples and said, "Say not ye, there are yet
four months, and then cometh the harvest? behold, I say unto
you. Lift up your eyes, and look on the fields, they are white
already unto harvest." This command seems to me to be very
timely for our people today. "Lift up your eyes."

Why do we not lift up our eyes? The reason is that our
eyes are fastened on the things of the world. There stands

a man with a dollar in his hand. His eyes are fastened stead-fastly on it. He does not lift them to see the opportunity to turn the dollar to the best account. While pressing men of this class to render unto the Lord that which is His, I have been asked, "Where is the Lord's post office?" To this I re-plied, "Wherever there is one who is in need, there God has a post office." Jesus said, "Inasmuch as ye did it unto one of these least, ye did it unto me." Why should Rockefeller, Carnegie, or we with our pittance, hesitate as to where we should invest our money so as to realize the greatest dividends? Austin Phelps says, "Vigilance is in watching opportunity; tact and daring, in seizing upon opportunity." Never was oppor-tunity greater for people of means than it is today.

II. God's purpose in our lives and our responsibilities for our opportunities.

This thought is suggested by the second part of the text: "Let us work that which is good." It is, or should be, an im-portant matter with us as to what we do with what God has given us. In giving us opportunities He has done it with a definite purpose and He will require their value at our hands. So, then,

1. Let us buy them up. We take this statement from Paul's language in Ephesians 5:16 and Colossians 4:5. In the body of the text they read: "Redeeming the time"; in the margin, "Buying up the opportunity." The word here translated "op-portunity" is the same as the one in our text. The word trans-lated "buying up" means "to save from being wasted," "to make the most of." It is evident that these passages refer only to present time and not to lost opportunities. We should enter the doors as they are opened to us.

2. This part of the text sets forth the positiveness of religion. Christianity has its positives as well as its negatives. Some people have what Sam Jones calls "gate-post" religion. They flatter themselves that they are religious because they do not steal, lie, swear, nor kill. Even the gate-post has the same of which to boast. The man who would convince the world that he is a Christian, let him show the spirit of our Lord, of whom it was said, "He went about doing good." It was this that con-vinced Nicodemus that he was a teacher "come from God."

So if we would convince the world that we are God's children, we must do it by the positiveness of our religion. It is common to hear the remark, "There is a good man," referring only to the man's negative goodness. It is not true. Men only are good who do good.

3. To this end we were created and recreated. I cannot conceive of a purpose of our existence in the world other than to glorify God. To this end He created man, and the Scriptures expressly declare that to this end we were recreated: "We are his workmanship, created in Christ Jesus for good works, which God afore prepared that we should walk in them." Again, Paul speaking of Christ, said, "Who gave himself for us, that he might redeem us from all iniquity, and purify unto himself a people for his own possession, zealous of good works." God saves people to serve him. This is the one divine purpose of our lives.

4. Let us look at a present condition. We have the name of being one of the best associations of the state. That is possible and probable, but we certainly cannot be satisfied with the compliments we receive. There are about seven thousand Baptists in this great county, and two or three thousand do all that is done in the name of this association. There are too many deserters in our Baptist army. It occurs to me that there is a great need for a course in court martialing and shooting. A man has no more right to desert a Baptist army in the heat of battle than he has to desert Uncle Sam in his conflict with the Spaniards or Filipinos. They are enrolled but not enlisted. O, for the power to enlist our people!

5. The unit of this organized force is the church. To the extent we ignore the development of the churches, to that extent we are weak. This text was written to the churches of Galatia. To this end Christ organized the church and died for it. The church that loses sight of the purpose of her existence has no right to exist.

Now let us consider

III. The extent and application of opportunities.

"Toward all men." This phase of the text recognizes

1. The relation that exists between all men. If there is a thing or being in the universe to which we bear no relation, then

toward that thing or being we owe no duty. I do not believe in the universal fatherhood of God, because Jesus said to a certain class of people to whom he preached, "Ye are of your father, the devil." But I do believe in the universal brotherhood of man as descended from a common parent. Wherever we meet one of Adam's posterity, we meet a brother. Our duty toward him is measured by the relation we sustain to him. This is plainly set forth by our Lord in his answer to the question, "Who is my neighbor?" in which he shows that this duty does not arise from race or nationality, but exists even between those who are at enmity.

2. It excludes selfishness. It is a lamentable fact that some of God's children have never arisen to the plane from which they can see beyond their own selfish interests and let their hearts throb in unison with their brethren for one common cause, even the cause of Christ. We should keep in mind that what we do in this selfish spirit is an abomination to God.

3. It sets forth the true idea of altruism. By this we mean the doctrine of "otherism." Often we hear it said that the Golden Rule is the true standard of life. Not so; it only purports to be a rule of reciprocation. By this rule we have as many standards as we have ideals of life; each one is to do to the other according to his own wish. Jesus came "not to be ministered unto, but to minister." We show His spirit in us by ministering to others. He said to His disciples, "A new commandment I give unto you, that ye love one another even as I have loved you." Here He makes His love the standard. We are wonderfully impressed with its meaning as we view the tragedy of the cross. There we see the righteous dying for the unrighteous. Even so, God is calling His people to the duty of giving their lives for a lost world. It is true that God calls just one here and there to die for His cause, but the greater call is to live for His cause. It is easier to die for Christ than it is to live for Him.

You ask, "Are we not to do good for ourselves?" I answer, that the higher purpose of life calls us to consider the needs of others, and the good we would do for ourselves should subserve the one great purpose to serve others. We are better enabled to do this as we consider the common fate of all. The poet has condensed it thus:

"The boast of heraldry, the pomp of power,
All that beauty, all that wealth e'er gave;
Await alike, the inevitable hour—
The paths of glory lead but to the grave."

This was recited by General Wolfe as he crossed the St. Lawrence the day before the Battle of Quebec. But I would rather have it said of me, "He went about doing good," than to have the laurels of Wolfe, Napoleon, or Alexander the Great. Their reward was of this world; ours is eternal.

4. It sets forth the missionary idea. I would not come before this intelligent body of Baptists with a message so limited in scope that I could not discuss the subject of missions without digression. I have the honor of being called a missionary by my churches. Some of my members inquire, "When are you going to let up on this missionary question?" I answer, "When Christ comes." If there is anything that characterizes us as a people, it is the fact that we are missionary. In this we are more like our Lord than in being Baptists. "As we have opportunity, let us work that which is good toward all men." In what can we do more good to a people than to give them the Gospel? Notice how broad the text in its application. "Toward all men." Christ died for the Hottentot, as He did for you and me. If we have the spirit of Christ, we will love them for whom He died. This is one of the greatest tests of our love.

5. The last thought is that our responsibility is co-extensive with our opportunities. The one who has neglected an opportunity to do good will never know his loss until he faces it in the eternal beyond. Lost opportunities will be thorns in our dying pillows. It is at the end that we shall look back over our lives to see the lost opportunities, which cause an expression of sadness to overshadow our brows; and if our friends inquire if we are afraid, we shall answer as did the dying young man who had done nothing for his Lord, "No; I am not afraid; Jesus saves me now, but oh, must I go and empty-handed?" "Alas! The number who will realize the truth of the poet with multiplied intensity:

"Of all sad words of tongue or pen,
The saddest are these: 'It might have been.'"

But with those who have been faithful to the trust committed to them, it will not be so. "They shall shine as the brightness of the firmament—and as the stars forever and ever."

CHAPTER VII

J. B. GAMBRELL

BIOGRAPHICAL SKETCH*

James Bruton Gambrell, descendant of French Huguenots, was born in Anderson County, South Carolina, August 21, 1841. When he was four years old his parents moved to northeast Mississippi.

Each day the father read the Bible, and he or an old Negro slave led in prayer. The family attended the Pleasant Ridge Church, the father missing only two Saturday meetings in twenty-five years. As a lad he was greatly influenced by reading a book, *Facts for Boys,* which he bought from a colporter for two dimes, the proceeds from the sale of two coon skins. He faced the decision between books and dogs, chose books, and borrowed and read all he could find.

He was converted at the age of fifteen and joined the Pleasant Ridge church. Determining to get an education he enrolled in a school taught by Professor R. M. Leavell at Cherry Creek when the war of the '60's began. He enlisted in the company organized by his teacher, Captain Leavell, and was sent to Virginia where he served first as a member of Pickett's division at Gettysburg, and later as a scout for Robert E. Lee. He was transferred to the Memphis section, where as captain, he organized and commanded a company of scouts. Returning to the Suffolk section in Virginia he married, on January 13, 1864, Miss Mary T. Corbell, a cousin of Mrs. George E. Pickett. They went to Mississippi to live in the latter part of 1866.

His first impression to preach came while in Mississippi. In December, 1866, he was licensed by the church where he

*By Dr. E. C. Routh, Editor "The Commission", Baptist Foreign Mission Board.

had been converted. In November, 1867, he was ordained by the Cherry Creek Church which he and Mrs. Gambrell had joined while teaching school at Wallerville. He counseled with General Mark P. Lowrey on the founding of Blue Mountain College. In 1870 he became pastor of the West Point church. Two years later he accepted the call of the Oxford Church and enrolled in the University of Mississippi. He attended his first Southern Baptist Convention at Charleston, South Carolina, in 1874.

In February, 1877, the *Baptist Record* was projected and he was asked to become editor. He served in that position fifteen years. During the greater part of that time he lived at Clinton where Mississippi College is located, served as pastor of the church and did field work for the college. As editor he fought against saloons. His oldest son, Roderick Dhu, publisher of a prohibition publication, was assassinated in that fight.

In 1891 at Birmingham, Dr. Gambrell and Dr. J. M. Frost were appointed a sub-committee on establishing the Sunday School Board, and after a full day of prayerful deliberation, submitted a report which led to the beginning. He was elected president of Mercer University in 1893. He resigned at the end of three years and agreed to accept the nomination of the Populist Party for governor of Georgia if it would declare for prohibition, but was ineligible because not a resident of the state six years.

In December, 1896, he began his greatest work as Secretary of Texas Baptists. They had reached a critical juncture due to division on the missionary program. Under his wise and tactful leadership they were unified. He said, "More people, a hundred to one, will join in a bear hunt than will turn out to kill a mouse." More than any other he set the pattern for a constructive co-operative plan of missionary work in Texas and the South. Under his leadership evangelistic efforts were expanded, the Baptist Education Commission constituted, the Texas Baptist Memorial Sanitarium built, and the Southwestern Baptist Theological Seminary established.

On February 10, 1910, he resigned as Secretary to accept the editorship of the *Baptist Standard* serving until December, 1914, when, following the consolidation of the state Mission and Education Boards he was elected Executive Secretary. For nearly four years he led Texas Baptists in their enlarged program.

During the World War period, characterized by tensions and discussions concerning Southwide boards, Dr. Gambrell was elected president of the Southern Baptist Convention at New Orleans and served four years. He handled a typically acute situation with gavel in hand, by saying, "Don't forget, brethren, that a hot box slows up the train." At the Atlanta Convention in 1919, when the Convention was invited to join the Inter-Church World Movement, Dr. Gambrell said: "Baptists never ride a horse without a bridle." He was famous for his aphorisms and stories, especially dog stories.

In June, 1918, he asked to be relieved of his heavy duties as Secretary and took up the professorship of Christian Ethics and Ecclesiology in Southwestern Seminary, to which he had given some time each week while editor-in-chief of the *Standard*. He continued thus until his death.

One of the most distinctive contributions of Dr. Gambrell was his European trip in 1920 with Drs. Mullins, Truett, Love. They attended a conference of European Baptists in London in July which resulted in the expansion of the Southern Baptist Missions to include Spain, Jugoslavia, Hungary, Rumania, Ukraine, and Palestine-Syria. He went on through Europe visiting practically all countries except Russia. Quite a trip for the veteran nearing his eightieth year!

A little while after he returned, his physical heart faltered for the first time. From his sick bed he sent his last message to the Southern Baptist Convention saying: "Do right and go forward." Then came the end of his earthly journey, June 10, 1921. We can still hear him saying to Southern Baptists: "Do right and go forward."

UP FOOL HILL*

Fool Hill lies just where the undulating lowlands of boyhood rise sharply up to the highlands of manhood. It is climbed only by big boys and the big boy is an institution in this world. He is, indeed, a series of personalities in one extraordinary combination. The only certain thing about him is his uncertainty. Like a spit-devil, he is loaded, and will go off with a spark, but just which way he will go is an unknown and an unknowable thing. But the chances are that he will go zigzag, and whichever way he does go you can trace him by the sparks.

When you notice the boy feeling of his upper lip, and a suspicious of something slightly darker than the skin appears, you may begin then to look sharp. The boy has come to the foot of fool hill, and will begin very soon to climb. The great problem is to get him up the hill in good repair. That done, you have blessed the world with a man.

Big boys are nearly certain to have the big-head. This is no bad sign. It is an inward sense of power, without the wisdom of discipline. Our boy entering the fool age is a caution. His voice is now fine and splitting, now coarse and grating. He begins a sentence coarse and ends fine, or fine and ends coarse. He is rank and sets digging to the world. All his judgments are pronounced and final. There is nothing he cannot decide instanter. He knows instantly and by intuition who is the greatest lawyer in the whole country, if he is a reading boy, or the best doctor. He can tell you who will be the next governor or anything else politicians are so anxious to know. He is authority on prize-fights, or cards, or anything else he knows nothing about. And when he pronounces on anything he has spoken. The governor is "Dick" somebody, and the supreme judge is "Tom". And, by the way, he often differs with these and other dignitaries. He sings in unearthly strains, with tendencies to the pathetic and the savage all in one breath.

With the big boy there is nothing medium. He uses adjectives freely and always in the superlative. He sees things in strong colors, for he is in the flood of passion. Fight! Yes, fight anything and on the shortest notice. He ought to fight to prove himself, so he feels. About this time his mind undergoes

*From *Parable and Precept* by J. B. Gambrell, Fleming H. Revell. Used by permission.

some radical changes. He wonders at the dullness and con-
trariness of his parents. It is a constant worry to him that he
can't manage his father without a world of trouble, and he wonders what is the matter with "the old man" anyhow. Churches
and Sunday schools are too dull for him, and the preacher is
just nowhere. He can give him any number of pointers on theology and preaching.

Rushing on and into everything like mad, he stops short and
bewails the coldness of this unfriendly world. Now he has
more "dear friends" than he can shake a stick at; now he feels
that he has not a friend in the world. He wants sympathy, while
he tries the patience of everybody who has anything to do with
him.

Such is the boy in the fool age. The great question is, what
to do with him. He is climbing "fool hill" now, and the road is
bad. Father, mother and friends are all anxious and sometimes vexed. Homes are deprived of all their peace by this
great double-action marplot. But the question will not down.
What shall we do with him? If he is turned loose now, he will
be a wild engine on the track smashing things. If he is not
handled wisely there will be a catastrophe. The ever-recurring
question is: What shall be done with the big boy climbing fool
hill? Often the impulse is to let the fool go. But that will not
do. He is now like a green apple—sour, puckerish and unwholesome; but, like the apple, if we can save him, he will ripen
into something good. We must save him. Saints and angels,
help us to save this human ship in the storm, freighted with
father's, mother's, sister's, brother's love, and with the infinite
wealth of an immortal nature! We must save him for himself,
his loved ones and his country.

The chances for saving him will depend mainly on what
has been done for him before he struck fool hill. If, from in-
fancy, he has been taught to revere sacred things, if he has been
taught subjection to authority, if his mind has been stored with
scripture texts, with noble poems, and recollections of the pure,
the sweet, the good, you have in him the saving elements. We
must never forget that in the final analysis every person saves
or loses himself, no matter what influences help or hinder. A
well-taught boy may climb this dubious hill without a bobble,

but if the new life gains the temporary lead the chances are that the enduring good elements will reassert themselves and become paramount. Hence the transcendent importance of ballasting this ship betimes, before the storm sets in. Noble ambitions early planted and carefully nurtured are of great importance. During this period of trial, great wisdom and tact are needed. There must be a gradual lengthening of the ropes. If you tie this mustang up too tight he will break the rope, and maybe break his neck. It often happens that more can be done by indirection than otherwise. Some good woman, other than the boy's mother, may be a savior to him.

He feels his great importance, and you must recognize him. It is just here that the churches have failed and the saloons have succeeded. Show this embryonic governor that you recognize his parts and call on him for service. The harder the service the better he will like it. Get in with him, and do not be too critical, but pass his imperfections by. He will be nearly everything, but never mind; he only sees things large and sees them double and mixed, being now partly boy and partly man, and seeing with two sets of eyes.

You are fighting the devil for a soul, and you can't afford to be impatient, or give way to anger, when your fool boy takes an extra flounce. When he gets on a bad bent, give line, as the fisherman does when there is a hundred-pound tarpon on the other end of the line, but not too much. And remember all the while that time and heaven are on your side. With age comes discretion. Once up fool hill the road stretches away ever smoother and better to the pearly gates.

Our big boy is among us. His folly breaks into dudishness. He is an unturned cake, but likely there is good substance in him. He is worth cooking. If you see him on the street, take him by the hand and say a good word to him. His mother will be glad of it. Look him up and ask him to your house. Reach after his heart, for he has one. Two worlds are interested in that young fool, and underneath his folly there lies sleeping maybe a great preacher, teacher or other dignitary of the commonwealth.

CONSIDERING CIRCUMSTANCES AND CONDITIONS

"Overlooking fields" and "considering circumstances and conditions", have come to be vocational. We have people who do little else. Some of them have risen to the dignity of "experts." Others have become ministerial tramps, fleeing from place to place on account of "circumstances and conditions." So much do some dwell on "circumstances and conditions" that they have become enslaved to them.

Many of this class have trained their minds to see only the bad "circumstances and conditions". They "look over a field," see every bad thing, and make a map of the difficulties in their minds for future use. I know a preacher who has so bent his mind to this dolorous task that he can see nothing but difficulties in any place. He is not a pastor now. There were so many "circumstances and conditions" everywhere, that he quit, and the churches now have rest. No pulpit ought to sound like a frog pond. People won't hear a croaker long. The people have sense.

The tribe I am considering came down from antiquity. We read of them in Holy Writ The ten spies who took the heart out of Israel by reporting on the "circumstances and conditions" in the "Promised Land" were whipped by what they saw. The long-necked giants were a part of the circumstances. Only two of the spies could see above the "circumstances and conditions." They saw God and the promises. The ten were completely enslaved by the sight of their eyes and all their strength oozed out. They were in their own eyes as grasshoppers.

Another example of mental and spiritual subjugation to "circumstances and conditions" was the army of Israel when Goliath dared them. This great giant, and his big spear and loud mouth were circumstances that brought on a condition of fear, weakness and cowardly submission.

All Israel had the buck ague when David arrived. He gave very little time to "looking over the field", or considering "circumstnces and conditions." It was plain enough that these were bad. As Dr. Carroll would say, "the people were whipped inside." David, in the name of the Lord, took a rock and knocked Goliath in the head in quick order.

All the "circumstances and conditions" were the worst in the storm and shipwreck Paul was in. Paul got in connection with God and they all changed for good. What a blessing one brave soul is when "circumstances and conditions" are bad!

In religious matters the habit of forming conclusions from a mere human view of "circumstances and conditions" is utterly enslaving. The scheme of progress in religion as recorded in the Scriptures, implies a power above the human level, which changes "circumstances and conditions".

Materialist and near-sighted scientists are engaged in a huge effort to evolve the universe from the "circumstances and conditions" of matter. The true explanation of the material world is in the first sentence in the Bible: "In the beginning was God." God is the explanation of all religious success, as well as of creation,—not "circumstances and conditions."

There was a divided church, wasted and prostrated by internal wars. Several brethren went and "looked over the field." After considering the "circumstances and conditions" they said nothing could be done. The remnants were poor and without influence. The other people in town were strong and respectable. No one of standing would go about the little old neglected church. The "circumstances and conditions" made it impossible to do anything. They were very wise men of a very religiously ignorant sort.

Later came a young man who had a favorite text. "Have Faith in God." He never feared "circumstances or conditions." If he saw them nobody knew it. He preached and all prayed. God conquered and the "circumstances and conditions" didn't seem to amount to anything. The people flocked where God was. There is a great church there today.

"Circumstances and conditions" were very bad when Israel was at the Red Sea, but what difference did it make when God stretched out His mighty arm?

The burgomaster of Hamburg said to Oncken when Baptists in Germany were few and weak and persecuted: "As long as I can raise my finger I will put you down." With Germany against Oncken, the "circumstances and conditions" were very bad. Oncken replied to the burgomaster, "And as long as I can see God above your finger, I will preach." There are many

Baptists in Germany today. When God is in a situation "circumstances and conditions" conform to His will.

Two preachers went to a place in Texas to hold a meeting. They were told it was no use. Others had tried and failed. The people did not care for religion. There was one man there who would upset things, a sort of Goliath of Gath. The preachers paid no attention to "circumstances and conditions," but sailed in with the sword of the Spirit. Goliath was converted and scores of others. The "circumstances and conditions" were all changed gloriously.

Spurgeon wanted a great preaching place in London. But the people and most of the deacons said, "considering the circumstances and conditions' we can't build it. We are poor and have not the money." Spurgeon and six deacons prayed it out before God and triumphed in faith. A little later Spurgeon received $80,000 and never did know who sent it. The house was built, and "circumstances and conditions" improved steadily.

Near where I was raised was a community that was known as the worst "devil's den" in the country. It would have been the delight of the modern "sociological expert." There was the making of a book in it. A worse set of "circumstances and conditions" could not be found. A country preacher, after laying by his crop, took a Bible and hymn book and went to work. The devil's crowd cut saddles and bridles to pieces, shot guns around the meeting place at night, told the preacher to leave, but he cried to God and went on. In three weeks the devil's patch was cleaned up. Multitudes were converted and baptized, among them the leader of the devil's forces, and to-day the "circumstances and conditions" in that country are fine.

No man is going to earn his salt as a preacher if he can't see higher than "circumstances and conditions." The spirit of the times is trying to enslave the Christian world by involving its faith and everything in the doctrine of "circumstances and conditions." It is a cheat and a lie. God will make all things new by a power eternal in Himself. In these days of weakening faith the passing word in religion is that mighty word of Scripture, Power. Not influence, not education, but power, the power that brought Jesus from the dead, is to conquer. Without this power we are no-bodies in religion. With it "circumstances and conditions" are mere incidents of victory.

I say it with deep conviction, the supreme need of this age is the emancipation of the minds of men from "circumstances and conditions" and lifting of their minds to God, as the source of victory. Think of Paul's great words: "I can do all things through Christ who strengtheneth me." We must never get away from faith in the immanence of the divine in our work. Get down your Bible and read and ponder the eleventh chapter of Hebrews again and see how faith ranged above the "circumstances and conditions" in the days gone. These things were written for your instruction.

The subject draws me out. We must have the faith that dominates "circumstances and conditions" in order to have courage. My pencil point is now at the weakest place in the religious life of today. The "circumstances and conditions" are in modern life like the "perlice" in the story my good friend, Dr. Bernard, of Georgia, told of Irish bravery. An Irishman was saying that there were 100,000 as brave Irishmen as ever lived ready right then to fight for liberty. "Well, why don't they fight?" was asked. "They are afeard of the perlice," was the reply.

Preachers fear "circumstances and conditions." We must come back to simple faith and direct, personal effort. Waiting for "circumstatnces and conditions" to favor effort will never win. The farmer who keeps one eye on the clouds and the other on the wind will not make a crop. The farmer who industriously plows and plants and cultivates, believing in God and trusting Him for the increase will rarely have to buy corn. Walking by the sight of our eyes in religion will make pigmies of us all. We are to walk by faith, not by sight. It was because Moses saw Him who was invisible that he lived his wonder life.

If some preachers do not take a good steady look up, they are going to let "circumstances and conditions" keep them from taking collections. They will give down just when they ought to be strong in the Lord and in the power of His might. They will play the coward and begin a process of weakening within their own hearts, with God and the people. They will be "looking over another field" soon. Now is the time to rise above "circumstances and conditions" like men of God and do exploits.

CHAPTER VIII

A. H. NEWMAN

BIOGRAPHICAL SKETCH*

Reflection upon the life of Dr. Newman raises a baffling problem. Are some individuals placed in the course of history to perform specific tasks? It would seem that Paul was such an one. Martin Luther, Thomas Jefferson and Abraham Lincoln are other examples. Any time if crisis will call forth men of high ability who constitute the leaders of the age. It is interesting that the state of Georgia, just after the Civil War, produced a number of such personalities.

Dr. Newman, America's leading church historian, was born in the Edgefield District of South Carolina in 1852. His father was a farmer and harness maker who moved to Georgia after the Civil War. Young Albert learned to read at three. Later he was taught by several men, the most important being the Rev. E. A. Steed, a brilliant but somewhat eccentric man. Young Newman was so acquisitive that he was able to enter the junior year of Mercer University at seventeen and to graduate at the head of the class a few months before he was nineteen.

In 1872 he entered the Rochester Theological Seminary where he specialized in Hebrew and Old Testament Exegesis and graduated in May, 1875. The next year he studied Hebrew under Dr. Toy and New Testament Greek under Dr. Broadus at the Southern Baptist Seminary. He had extraordinary retentiveness, singular ability to acquire dead languages and undying devotion to truth.

In the fall of 1876 he returned to Rochester where he was made professor of Church History. In 1881 Dr. Newman transferred to Toronto Baptist College which later became McMaster

*By Dr. Frederich Eby, Professor of History and Philosophy of Education, University of Texas.

University. First at the Rochester Seminary and then more fully at McMaster he found his task. With superb gifts for language he set about mastering the history of Christianity reading the original sources in Greek, Latin and German. It was the history of the origin and doctrines of the Baptists that presented his most unique opportunity.

Newman's ability as a scholar came to be recognized in a rather interesting way. In 1885 the fourth volume of Dr. Philip Schaff's monumental *History of the Christian Church* appeared Dr. Newman reviewed this book for the *Baptist Quarterly Review*. Dr. Schaff took him to task for some of his Scriptures, but nevertheless recognizing his exceptional scholarship, and invited him to edit St. Augustine's treatises on anti-Manicheanism. Some of these treatises had to be translated from the Latin by Dr. Newman himself. This work gave him a permanent place among the first scholars of the day.

At the suggestion of Dr. Newman the American Society of Church History promoted a series of histories of the Protestant denominations in the United States. He was invited to participate and in 1894 published his *History of the Baptist Churches in the United States*. No one had ever attempted to bring together in orderly fashion the facts of the opposition to infant baptism. This he did in *A History of Anti-pedo-baptism from the Rise of Pedo-baptism to 1609*, which was published in 1897.

The next effort was to write the history of the Christian Church. These two impartial volumes, written in splendid style, have been used as texts in many Baptist seminaries and also seminaries of other denominations. Just at the close of the century Dr. Newman with the colaboration of a group of leaders produced *A Century of Baptist Achievement*. This work laid the foundation for the establishment of the Baptist World Alliance which held its first session in London in 1905.

In 1901 Dr. Newman was asked by Dr. B. H. Carroll and President Oscar H. Cooper to assist them in building a great theological seminary at Baylor University. The Baptists of Texas were growing in numbers and wealth with unparalleled rapidity. The cities were increasing in population and culture. The large and cultured congregations demanded not only good but scholarly men as pastors. A seminary was imperative if Texas Baptists were to hold their people and advance. Dr. Newman saw the extraordinary opportunity and accepted the offer.

He gave up his teaching at Southwestern in 1913 and returned to Baylor where he gave a course in Church History. During 1917-18 he was visiting professor of Comparative Religion at Vanderbilt University. In 1921 President Rufus W. Weaver of Mercer University turned to Dr. Newman to assist him in developing a school of theology at that institution. He taught during the summer sessions at the University of Chicago, and finally closed his career by returning to McMaster University for the session of 1927-28.

Dr. Newman married Mary Augusta Ware, the daughter of a well-to-do plantation owner of Seale, Alabama, in 1873. Four children constituted the family: Dr. H. H. Newman, an authority in research, was Professor of Zoology at the University of Chicago until his retirement. The only daughter, Elizabeth, married Frederick Eby and has lived for many years in Austin, Texas. Dr. Henry Ware Newman after some years as a missionary in China is in medical practice in Austin. The youngest son, Albert Broadus, is with the College of the City of New York, and leader in the field of Chemical engineering.

Dr. Newman died at the home of his daughter, June 4, 1933. Mrs. Newman died the following January. His work still lives.

THE AUTHORITY OF CHRISTIAN CONSCIOUSNESS

By "authority" we understand "legal or rightful power", a "right to command." The correlative idea is that of obligation to obey. The king has authority over his subjects, the general over his soldiers, the parent over his child. Such authority, however, is purely derivative in its nature and hence is not absolute. The king's authority does not extend to the thoughts or the conscience of his subjects. At the utmost he can command only external obedience; he cannot command internal accord.

The question is not one of authority derived and limited, but of authority absolute; not of a right of Christian Consciousness to control one department of man's being, but of a right to control man's entire being—body, soul and spirit. The only authority that pertains to man's entire being, and that is absolute and final, is *the will of God*. The question for discussion, therefore, is whether or not Christian Consciousness is a trustworthy and infallible expression of God's will.

The *a priori* probability that God would reveal His will in a way that should be readily apprehended by His children is generally admitted. Has He left man to the gropings of reason? The utter failure of reason throughout the ages to gain any sufficient idea of what it concerns us, as immortal, spiritual beings to know, seems decisive against this method. Is conscience a sufficient revealer of God's will? The immortality of mankind, on the one hand, and the utter despair, resulting in asceticism on the other, point to a negative answer. Reason demands truth, but cannot find it. Conscience demands righteousness, but cannot realize. Revelation—above all God's perfect revelation of Himself in the Incarnate Christ—fulfills the demands of reason and of conscience.

I. It's Meaning

What, now, is Christian Consciousness? Consciousness, I take it, is essentially man's immediate knowledge of his own acts and states, the latter term including the impressions made upon him by God and His creatures. Christian Consciousness is the consciousness of a Christian. The Christian Consciousness differs from ordinary human consciousness in so far as a regenerate man differs from an unregenerate. I have at-

tempted to define consciousness as a faculty; the term is likewise used to denote the deliverance of this faculty. The term
Christian Consciousness is capable of a like employment. By
a still further extension the term comes to designate the common
Christian sentiment with reference to the matter of which
Christian Consciousness takes cognizance. In this general sense
the Christian Consciousness of the present generation would be
the combined result of the Christian life and thought of the
past eighteen centuries, and the Christian life and thought of
the present.

Let us suppose a man combining in his own person all the
good and bad qualities of humanity, converted to Christ in the
apostolic time, subjected to the Judaizing processes of the early
centuries, plunged at last into the depths of mediaeval bigotry
and superstition, emancipated from bigotry and superstition
through the study of the Bible and the influence of Greek and
Arabic philosophy, subjected to the various influences of
Lutheran and Calvinistic Protestantism, precipitated in turn into Socinian rationalism and indifferentism, and into hyper-
Calvinistic fatalism, aroused thence into a state of frantic
evangelistic enthusiasm. In a word, let us suppose him to
have passed through every imaginable phase of Christian life
and thought, to be still alive and resting at present in some of
the multudinous religious parties. The experiences of the past
would remain and would form a part of the contents of his
Christian Consciousness.

The Divine element is permanent and unvarying. The impression made by the Divine element in consciousness will
depend very largely upon the character of the individual, upon
inherited and acquired capabilities and tendencies, and upon
environment. Each Christian individual has a Christian Consciousness different from that of every other individual. Each
age has a collective Christian Consciousness different from that
of any other age. So far as there is agreement it depends upon
the invariableness of the Divine element, likeness of natural
and acquired dispositions, a common using of the experience
of the past.

There are points in which Christians of all religious parties
agree, and in which universal Christian Consciousness may be

said to speak with one voice, but I am doubtful whether the contents of such a consensus would be very rich. There might be a considerable show of agreement in words, but the same form of words may express widely different conceptions in the minds of a number of individuals using it. We should expect that in those who are truly regenerate there would be agreement at least in the understanding of the fundamental truths of Divine revelation; but even here remarkable differences would appear.

For practical purposes, however, we are precluded from making use of the deliverances of the universal regenerate consciousness by the following considerations: 1. We cannot infallibly discriminate between the regenerate and the unregenerate. 2. Even in regenerate consciousness we cannot determine infallibly how much of consciousness is due to the regenerate principle, and how much is due to the natural man. 3. If these two difficulties were out of the way, it would be a practical impossibility to collect all these deliverances in such a way as to compare them. 4. Even if we had them collected and expressed in words, we could by no possibility determine the signification that any given form of words bore to the consciousness of each individual employing it. Practically, it is likely to mean, in the mouth of any individual user, the views that he and his set have come to entertain with reference to the great questions of theology, morals and religion.

The church historian can divide the eighteen Christian centuries into great epochs, and can characterize each epoch by a few general statements. If the middle ages are rightly characterized by intolerance, superstition and fanaticism; finding general expression in crusades, inquisition, and idolatry; the nineteenth century is no less characterized by tolerance, freedom from superstition and fanaticism, philanthrophy, scientific investigation, etc. Underlying the Christian life and thought of the middle ages, there must have been a general Christian Consciousness differing widely from that which underlies the Christian life and thought of the present. Philosophical views and scientific theories, while they are in part a product of the age in which they appear, exert in turn a vast influence upon the Christian Consciousness of the age.

II. It's Trustworthiness

How far and in what sense Christian Consciousness may be accepted as a trustworthy expression of the will of God. Here our best instructor will be the Word of God. To reach a satisfactory view of the relation between Christian Consciousness and the teaching of scripture as to the believer's special qualification for apprehending spiritual things, we should have a clear understanding of the scriptural representation of man in his unfallen, fallen, and regenerate states. I am inclined to accept the division of man's nature into body, soul, and spirit (*soma, psuche and pneuma*) as most in accord with scripture. and as best explaining the facts of man's unfallen, fallen, and regenerate states.

Psuche is the seat of personality, the immortal principle, and embraces intellect, emotion, and will. *Pneuma* is the Divine principle in man, manifesting itself chiefly in conscience, in aspirations after God, in communion with God, and in apprehension of spiritual things. In the unfallen man *soma* and *psuche* were under the control of *pneuma*. The subjection of *soma* and *psuche* to *pneuma* constituted man holy, and gave him blessed communion with God. The fall consisted in the fact that *psuche* emancipated itself from the control of *pneuma*, through which chiefly the will of God was made known. Though dethroned, *pneuma* persisted in the form of conscience and of a prompting toward godliness, more or less pronounced. *Psuche*, in so far as sensuality supplanted *pneuma* in its control, is represented as under the dominion of *sarx*. Yet the struggle between *pneuma* and *sarx* continues in the unregenerated man, intellect itself (*nous*), declaring the way of the *pneuma* to be the preferable way, but *sarx* prevailing over *pneuma*, and constituting the man *sarkical*.

When the unregenerated man is spoken of without special reference to his subjection to the *sarx*, he is said to be *psychical*. In regeneration man's *pneuma* is reinforced by the Divine *pneuma*, *sarx* is dethroned, and *psuche* and *soma* are brought under the dominion of the *pneuma*. Christ dwelling spiritually in the believer constitutes his true life. Yet the strivings of the *sarx* do not at once cease. Though it has received its death blow, it is tenacious of life. The believer does not once for all become what according to his profession he should be. The regenerate man is called *sarkical* or *psychical* on the other hand, and *spiritual* on the other, as the psychical or spiritual elements, including not mere sensuality, but a rebellious attitude of the intellect and will as well, are not, or are, in entire subjection to the spiritual. In the perfected state, *pneuma* becomes absolutely dominant, while in the finally impenitent *pneuma* remains as the Divine accuser, the "worm" that "dieth not."

What, then, shall we say of the authority of the conscious-ness of the regenerate man with reference to the things of God? The believer is said (I Cor. 2) to speak God's wisdom in a mystery, even the wisdom that hath been hidden. "We re-ceive . . . the spirit, which is of God; that we might know the things that are freely given to us by God." "He that is spiritual judgeth all things, and he himself is judged of no man. For who hath known the mind of the Lord, that he should instruct Him? But we have the mind of Christ." Believers are spoken of as "reflecting in a mirror the glory of the Lord," and are said to be "transformed into the same image from glory to glory." Believers are said to "have an anointing from the Holy One," and to "know all things." The Apostle *knew* whom he had believed. "If any man willeth to do His (God's) will, he shall know of the doctrine."

I think we may safely say, that if in any given cause we could be perfectly sure that the *sarx* is in complete subjection and that the *pneuma* is absolutely dominant, that we are filled with the Spirit, that we have realized as complete a union with Christ as it is the privilege of the believer to enjoy. If we could say without reservation "to me living is Christ," in such case, I doubt not, our Christian Consciousness would express God's will in a highly authoritative form.

But, alas! those of us who are not hopelessly eccentric know too well how the *sarx* is still within us, and how incomplete is dominion of *pneuma*. And we cannot escape the conviction, based on experience and observation, that Christian Conscious-ness, while it has its important place in furnishing the believer with assurance of his acceptance with God, and of the reality of his personal appropriation of revealed truth, is exceedingly *variable* and *deceptive*. I believe that just in proportion to the

height of the Christian's attainment in spiritual life will be his
lack of confidence in the infallibility of the deliverance of his
consciousness, and his sense of the need of a higher standard
of appeal.

III. It's Perversions

1. Gnosticism. We should be scarcely justified in regarding
the Gnostics of the first and second centuries as conscious de-
ceivers. Many of them were no doubt wholly sincere in the
belief that they had arisen above *pistis* to complete *gnosis,* and
that they had found in Christianity a key to the mystery of the
universe. Now no sane man of the present thinks that the
slightest degree of authority is to be attached to the Christian
Consciousness of a Basileides or a Valentinus. The fact is,
they were woefully deceived, and lured multitudes of souls to
destruction.

2. Montanism, in some respects the antithesis of Gnosticism,
furnishes a still better illustration of the deceptiveness of Christian Consciousness, because we feel surer of the sincerity of
its leading representatives, and because the movement involved
a more direct appeal to the authority of Christian Consciousness. Montanism represents, on the one hand, a reaction
against the growing secularization of the church and the speculative spirit of Gnosticism, and, on the other hand, a revival of
heathen manticism, with its wild enthusiasm, ecstasy, visions, etc.
Wrought up into a frenzy by zeal for reform, in view of the
speedy approach of the end of the age, the Montanists supposed
their fevered fancies to be the direct utterances of the promised
Paraclete, who was to guide into all truth. Does any one now
believe that Montanus and his prophetesses were inspired by
the spirit of God in their unscriptural utterances?

3. Mysticism is another form of unwholesome dependence on
Christian Consciousness widely different from either of those
mentioned. Disgusted with the emptiness of forms and cere-
monies and the corruption of church life, and imbued with semi-
pantheistic, Neo-Platonic conceptions of God, man and the
world, the mystic turned his thinking inward and sought fully
to realize union and communion with God. By dint of profound
and long-continued meditation men of strongly intuitional minds

were able to persuade themselves that they were so completely merged in Deity, that the deliverances of their consciousness were the very utterances of God. "God and I are one in knowing," wrote Master Eckart. "God's essence is His knowing, and God's knowing makes me know Him. Therefore is His knowing my knowing. The eye whereby I see God is the same eye whereby he seeth me. Mine eye and the eye of God are one eye, one vision, one knowledge, and one love ... The inner voice is the voice of God." Few we take it, would venture to maintain that the pantheistic, often senseless, utterances of an Eckart, or a Suso, or even the more moderate and thoroughly devout utterances of a Tauler or a George Fox, are authoritative exponents of the Divine will.

4. The New Theology. It is in connection with the method of religious thought popularly known as the "New Theology" that the term Christian Consciousness is now most frequently used. Socinianism, Kantian and Hegelian philosophies, Colleridgeanism, German Biblical Criticism, New England Transcendentalism—these and other modes of thought, interacting and overlapping each other, have had much to do with the formation of the Christian Consciousness of the Andover School. The Andover Christian Consciousness so magnifies the love of God and the mercy of God as to lose sight, in a measure, of Gods punitive justice and of God's holiness, which is "a consuming fire." To quote the words of an Andover theologican: "The Christian thought of the mercy of God our Heavenly Father, has felt itself restrained by certain limitations which it is claimed the Bible puts upon the offer of the gospel to mankind, until now it can not help asking if there are any members of the human family who are shut out from the opportunities of grace, any who are left to be treated simply according to their actual deserts."

Now I have great respect for the Andover theologians, but does it not seem just a little presumptuous in them to set up their own religious sentiments in the face of the united sentiment of the most devout minds in all ages, nay, in the face of the Scripture itself, and to claim that these sentiments are the deliverances of Christian Consciousness? I had far rather trust the Christian Consciousness of a Smyth or a Munger. If Paul

and John were Jews and had been subjected to the influences
of their age, Smyth and Munger are nineteenth century Amer-
icans and have been subjected to influences even more likely to
pervert their Christian Consciousness. Besides, the united
Christian Consciousness of eighteen centuries has attested the
special Divine inspiration of the Scriptures. When we hear of
the Christian Consciousness of an individual of a faction setting
itself up in opposition to Scripture, I think we are pretty safe
in suspecting that *sarx* is lurking in the background.

CHAPTER IX

JEFF D. RAY

BIOGRAPHICAL SKETCH*

Jeff D. Ray is a colorful, many-sided man. Among the various worthwhile activities, his teaching young preachers how to preach is outstanding. He held the chair of Homiletics and Pastoral Duties at Southwestern Seminary from 1907 to his retirement in 1944. During that time he taught probably 5,000 students.

Preaching is his passion and it is emotional, building up a crescendo of emphasis spiraling to a climax. He has preached in nearly every county seat on the 16 railroads running out of Fort Worth and in many other towns and cities. He has preached many convention, commencement, and other occasional sermons. He has conducted many revivals. The latest one (1947), at 86 years of age, was in Orange, Texas, resulting in the salvation of souls, rededicated lives and the setting up of family altars.

Dr. Ray is a great lover of Christ, his gospel and his churches. He has cherished a deathless devotion to friends, such as "Judge" Fred Freeman and Dr. B. H. Carroll, being with the former like David with Jonathan, and with the latter like Timothy to Paul. "Lee" Scarborough, "Marse George" Truett and many others shared his devotion. Hosts of younger men look on "Uncle Jeff" as a spiritual father. His affection for his family was that of an old time Southern gentleman.

Among his characteristics, frankness and sincerity loom large. If he thought a colleague wrong he could be severe with him but the next day be as thoroughly apologetic if he had reason to revise his judgment. Another prominent trait is ideal-

*By Dr. L. R. Elliott, Librarian Southwestern Baptist Theological Seminary.

ism. He loves truth, beauty and honor. He used never to lock his office nor keep a record of the books he loaned from his library. He has paid thousands of bills without keeping a receipt. When a younger friend indignantly asked why he paid one a second time he replied, "Son, in order that the ministry be not blamed."

He wields a facile pen. He has written *The Highest Office*, 1923; *The Country Preacher, B. H. Carroll*, and *Trouble*, 1929; *Expository Preaching*, and *Meant for Men*, 1939; *The Scarlet Sin*, 1942. In addition he has contributed articles to both the religious and secular press. For ten years he has been a writer for the Fort Worth Star-Telegram. His column, "Your Problems and Mine" is well and widely known. He has written many feature articles on Baptist Conventions, local Texas history, and travel experiences. His writing is concise, streamlined. His sentences go in a straigth line, moving directly to the conclusion.

He is an effective public reader of the written Word. Thousands of Baptist convention messengers remember his forceful reading of the Scriptures. In chapel he read the Bible, Shakespeare (whose writing he regards as next to the Bible) Poe's "Raven", Longfellow's "Hiawatha" and other dramatic pieces. His purpose was to present truth through word pictures to the imagination as well as through logic to the reason.

Jefferson Davis Ray was born in Victoria, Texas, Nevember 24, 1860. His father fell in the War between the States. His mother, who was Ava Dollahite, heroically struggled against poverty to rear her children. He received a diploma from the National School of Oratory, Philadelphia, 1879, the A.B. from Baylor in 1882 and the D.D. in 1903. Other study was in the Southern Baptist Theological Seminary, 1895-97, and two summers in the University of Chicago.

His first wife, "the mother of my children," was Josephine Wood, whom he married in 1885. She died in 1918. Two children survive: Attorney Carroll Ray and Mrs. Josephine Freeman. His second wife was the dainty daughter of the old South, Lillian Spight. They were married in 1922 and she died in 1937. In 1938 he persuaded "Miss Georgia" Miller to resign as Dr. Scarborough's secretary and share his life and home.

He was ordained to the gospel ministry in 1882 and has served as pastor of Baptist Churches at Huntsville, Texas, 1882-85, 1889-95; Eminence, Kentucky, 1895-97; Caldwell, Texas, 1897-1901; Corsicana, Texas, 1901-03; Seventh and James Street Church, Waco, Texas, 1903-07. In 1886-89 he was director of Texas Baptist Sunday School and Colportage work. He was Baptist camp pastor at Camp Bowie, Fort Worth, during World War. I.

Dr. Ray is an humble man. He does not carry himself with the air of importance nor seems to realize that many Texas Baptists regard him as a prince of Israel. His famous dream underlines this trait. He dreamed that Dr. Truett and Dr. Scarborough had come to sojourn at his home. The time of their departure arriving his mother sent him to bridle and saddle their horses and hold them while the distinguished guests mounted and rode away. His well-remembered chapel speech, "Since I came," has deflated the ego of many a younger brother.

He has the insight to judge real rather than apparent values. When several names were mentioned for a vacant professorship and one seemed to gain the ascendency Dr. Ray remarked, "All the fine things you have said about this man are so. He knows more and can do less with it than any man you have named." When Baylor conferred the D.D. degree on him a brother chided him for his vanity. Dr. Ray replied: "Yes, Tom, I accepted the degree because the school I love and help wanted to show their appreciation. Nobody has paid attention to it and I have never referred to it. You refused a degree and have gone over the country bragging about it. Which of us is vain?"

Dr. Ray's hobby is working cross-word puzzles, and his recreation is walking. He probably participated in more Texas Baptist history than any man living. He is an honored and appreciated statesman. His influence for truth and righteousness reaches beyond the borders of time.

CHRIST'S REDEMPTION*

Text: "The redemption that is in Christ Jesus." Romans 3:24.

This text deals with a fundamental doctrine. Without the redemption that is in Christ Jesus religion offers no permanent basis for peace or joy, and no adequate motive for wholehearted service. Today I shall seek to show how the redemption in Christ touches us at four vital points: First, in giving us a new standing before God. Second, in giving us a new condition in the sight of God. Third, in giving us a new character from God. Fourth, in giving us a new fellowship with God.

I. A New Standing Before God.

Man's normal standing before God is expressed in the third chapter of John and the 18th verse: "He that believeth not is condemned already because he hath not believed in the name of the only begotten Son of God." Again in the 36th verse of the same chapter: "He that believeth not the son shall not see life, but the wrath of God abideth on him." And again, in the third chapter of Galatians, at the 10th verse: "They that are of the works of the law are under a curse, for it is written: Cursed is every one that continueth not in all the things that are written in the book of the law to do them."

We find for these scriptures that normally a man stands before God under the burden of condemnation, the weight of His curse, and the blight of His wrath, but the redemption that is in Christ Jesus gives him a new standing before God. We are delivered by this redemption from the weight of God's condemnation, for we find it set down at Romans 8:1 :"There is, therefore, now no condemnation to them that are in Christ Jesus." It removes the blight of God's wrath, for we find it said in First Thessalonians, the 5th chapter and 9th verse: "God hath not appointed us (that is, the believers) to wrath, but to obtain salvation by our Lord Jesus Christ." And it removes the weight of God's curse, for we find it written in Galatians 3:13: "Christ hath redeemed us from the curse of the law, being made a curse for us in our place."

You have read in *Les Miserables,* Victor Hugo's great

---

*Convention Sermon, Baptist General Convention of Texas, Nov. 8, 1902.

work, the story of the French peasant who was cast from his
cart and pinned beneath its wheels. A crowd of men gathered
about and were vainly seeking to deliver the unfortunate team-
ster. Jean Valjean, once a convict in the galley ships, now the
honored mayor of the city, comes upon the scene, and seeing
that without immediate relief his fellow man is soon to be
crushed to death, cast himself upon his breast and crawled in
under the loaded cart, and with almost super-human strength
lifted it from the unfortunate peasant and held it there until
he struggled out free.

I was that peasant, crushed to death beneath the weight of
sin. Jesus Christ was my Jean Valjean casting Himself in great
humiliation upon the earth and bore for me the weight of sin
and condemnation that crushed me down. He placed himself
in my place of jeopardy, that I might stand in His place of liberty, that it might be fulfilled which was spoken by Isaiah the
prophet: "Surely he hath carried our sorrows; he hath borne our
griefs. . . The Lord hath laid on him the iniquity of us all."

II. A New Condition in the Sight of God.

My next point is that the redemption that is in Jesus Christ
gives a new condition in the sight of God. Man's normal condition is one of uncleanness. Isaiah, the first chapter says: "The
whole head is sick; the whole heart is faint; from the sole of the
foot unto the head there is no soundness in it, but wounds and
bruises and putrifying sores." Paul in the first chapter of Romans says: "Wherefore God gave them up to uncleanness
through the lusts of their flesh."

Jesus Christ found me with the open token of sin upon my
breast, like the unfortunate woman in the *Scarlet Letter* with
the letter A—initial letter in adultery—on her breast. But in
giving me a new standing before Him he did not doom me to go
into heaven with this token of sin visible to the angels and the
redeemed saints, but cleansed me from it. He did what patching
up, working over, and mere reforming can never do. So what
ocean waters cannot do for even what we call our slightest sin,
the blood of Jesus Christ is able to do for that which we consider the deepest sin.

It was this to which Zechariah referred: "In that day there

shall be open to the house of David and to the inhabitants of
Jerusalem a fountain for sin and uncleanness." Isaiah said:
"Come, let us reason together. Though your sins be as scarlet,
they shall be as white as snow. Though they be red like
crimson, they shall be as white as wool." It was the tasting
of this nectar that moved John to write: "And the blood of
Jesus Christ his Son, cleanseth from all sin", and to picture
the redeemed hosts as clothed in white garments.

It was this cleansing power of the blood of Jesus to which
Paul referred in the 5th chapter and 21st verse of Second
Corinthians, when he said: "He who knew no sin God hath
made to be sin in our place, that we might be the righteousness
of God in him." His power to cleanse led God to say in the
Psalms: "As far as the east is from the west, so far have I
removed your transgressions from you." How far is it from
here to the east? Travel with the cable's speed a million years,
you have not reached the east. How far is it from here to the
west? Travel with a ligntning sweep a million years and you
have not reached the west. What God means to say by that
text is this: That the believer in Jesus Christ, as He looks upon
that believer, has his sins removed from him by the limitless
space of two infinities.

III. A New Character from God.

But I say not only that the redemption in Jesus gives us a
new standing before God and a new condition in the sight of
God, but also a new character from God. Man's normal
character as it relates to God is that of open rebellion against
Him, for we find it written in the 107th Psalm: "Because they
rebelled against the words of God and condemned the counsel
of the most high." And in the colossal eighth of Romans:
"The carnal mind is enmity against God, is not subject to the
law of God, neither indeed can be." Now, the carnal mind
does not mean some awfully bad mind that only wicked people
have, but the mind with which all of us were born. We hear
some talk in these days about salvation by character. Now,
there is in scripture taught a salvation by character, not that
character that is the result of reforming the shattered fragments
of man's fallen nature; but that character that is imparted
through faith in Jesus Christ.

Salvation would be sadly incomplete if God had simply taken off my shoulders sin's burden, and washed from my heart sin's stain, and yet left in my heart the seeds of a nature fatally in love with sin. What were heaven to me if I shall be doomed to spend eternity there, out of rapport with God, loving the things that are evil? But we have a new character through Jesus Christ, and so Paul writes in Second Corinthians the 5th chapter: "Therefore if any man be in Christ Jesus he is a new creation. Behold, all things are passed away. All things are become new."

So the redemption that is in Christ Jesus, after lifting the cart of sin's burden that presses me down to death, and after washing the filth and mire of the streets from the garments that have been stained, gives a new nature, a new character from God. Zacchaeus was a tax tyrant, whose ear was deaf to the cry of the widow or the orphan's moan. One day he met Jesus in the thoroughfare and he believed in Him, and at once there was a change in his attitude to the suffering poor, for he said: "I give half my goods to feed the poor." At once there was a change in his thought about fair dealing between man and man, for he said: "If I have taken anything from any man by false accusation, behold, I restore it to him fourfold." He believed in Jesus and had received a new nature from Him, and he was but fulfilling the scripture that said: "It is no longer I that live, but Christ that liveth in me." It could be said of him: "He is a new creation." A similiar experience took place in the conversion of the Philippian jailor.

IV. A New Fellowship with God.

Now, brethren, the last point is that the redemption that is in Jesus Christ has wrought for us a new fellowship with God. Man's normal relation to God is not one of fellowship, for we find in the tenth chapter of Psalms: "The wicked through the pride of his countenance will not seek after God. God is not in all his thoughts." And we find it written in the second chapter of Ephesians: "At that time ye were without Christ, being aliens from the commonwealth of Israel, and strangers from the covenant of promise." So the Scriptures teach that man's normal condition is the condition of an alien and a stranger, and one who, when he looks upon his sins, instead of flying to God for forgiveness, flees from God as an avenging Nemesis.

We are not in fellowship with God by nature. We are aliens and strangers to God by nature. There is a fascinating fiction afloat which they call the universal fatherhood of God, and it teaches that all men are the children of God. Now, the Scriptures in every part of them stand squarely against any such fictitious assumption, however much it may appeal to the sentimental mind. "They that are the children of the flesh, these are not the children of God." Does that sound like the universal fatherhood of God for all men?" "But as many as received him, to them (and not to any others—to them) gave he power to become the sons of God." Paul says: "Ye are the children of God"—how? By a natural birth? By a sort of universal sentimental connection between us and the Creator? No. "Ye are the children of God through faith in the Lord Jesus Christ."

The man who, for whatever pretext or reason, rejects Jesus Christ, has no right to claim God as his father, and no right to call God his father. The Scriptures teach that the man that doeth unrighteousness is a child of the devil. The Scriptures teach that the men who sin are the children of wrath and not the children of God. Unless I mistake the signs of the times, the coming battleground of our Southern Baptists will find its scene just upon this doctrine. Gradually it is weaving its way into the teachings of many pulpits, and institutions of learning. Let our churches begin now to rid themselves of this heresy, if it exists, or to forearm themselves against it if they see it coming. Let all our preachers everywhere announce that God is the father only of the believer. Let every church steeple bear upon the banner that it floats to the breeze the motto: "No man is the son of God except as he has become such by believing in the Son of God."

Now, let us spend the few moments that shall be left in discussing the question of the blessings that flow to us from this redemption that is in Christ Jesus. For one thing this redemption blesses us when we mourn for sin. "As one whom his mother comforteth, so will I comfort you." There is one brought nigh unto us by the redemption that is in Christ Jesus more able to comfort than a mother, for when my father and my mother forsake me, then the Lord taketh me up.

But further than that, this redemption that is in Jesus Christ greatly comforts me when we come to the consideration of our own wickedness and unworthiness. Remembering all that God has done for us, recalling all his matchless mercies there comes a yearning impulse in our hearts to do something for him. Just as the little lad's paltry loaves and fishes fed the multitudes, so, out of the empty vessel that I shall bring, the feast of God's glory shall be supplied. We as well as Christ help to feed the hungry multitudes.

This redemption that is in Christ Jesus, and the fellowship that is built upon it, helps us when we come to face the unknown and uncertain future. You turn your face at the call of God's Spirit to a new and untried field, not knowing what awaits you there, except that experience and God's spirit teach you that hardship and toil and disappointment and suffering and homeless poverty await you there. But you go out, not as one who has no comfort, but you go out as one walking upon the clouds, upborne by the promise of God to those who go forth to preach his gospel: "Lo, I am with you always, even to the end of the world."

And so, brethren, when we look into the unknown future, the fellowship, the comradship, the presence of God—vouched to us by the presence of Christ—helps and comforts and buoys up our hearts. My tired little boy walking by me said: "I don't care if I do get tired, just so I am with you." I know not what the future holds for me; I know not what of homeless poverty; I know not what of sorrow and pain; I know not what of bereavement at the hand of death; I know not what of persecution from the wicked world; but this much I know, that in all I shall not be weary if Thou art with me.

But, further still, not only does this fellowship that is in Christ Jesus on account of his redemption, comfort us in the remnant of this life; but this fellowship comforts us in the hour of death. Israel's bard, realizing the fellowship of God in Jesus Christ, wrote: "Yea, though I walk through the valley of the shadow of death, I will fear no evil." No believer will ever die in the dark. It may be at midnight, and the natural eye may be glazed and sightless, but there shall be a supernal light, because it shall be the light of Him who bore our darkness that we might have His light. Darkness enveloped the cross when Jesus was crucified that light might flood the couch of the saint when he came to die. Thus, as he is my substitute in everything else, he will also be my substitute in bearing for me the otherwise darkness of the grave that I might have through him the everlasting light of his presence.

But, more still, the fellowship of God, based upon the redemption that is in Jesus Christ, helps us when we come to consider that unknown eternity. To every unbeliever, eternity is a leap in the dark. To every believer, eternity is but faith's taking hold of the hand of the Father and stepping out into undimmed light. Jesus said: "I go to prepare a place for you, and if I go and prepare a place for you, I will come again and receive you unto myself, that where I am there ye may be also." Heaven is where Jesus is just as happiness to a true wife is where her husband is. We tremble at the verge of eternity, but let us make the leap, and we shall find that underneath are the everlasting arms.

> "All hail the power of Jesus' name
> Let Angels prostrate fall,
> Bring forth the royal diadem,
> And crown Him Lord of all!
> Let every kindred, every tribe,
> On this terrestial ball,
> To him all majesty ascribe
> And crown Him Lord of all."

CHAPTER X

I. E. REYNOLDS

AUTOBIOGRAPHICAL SKETCH

I was born September 7, 1879, in Shades Valley, Alabama, five miles from Birmingham. Later we moved to a farm near Springville where I worked until I was twenty. I drove twenty-five miles in a wagon to Birmingham to secure work. My first job was carrying shingles at fifty cents per day. Later I built gin brushes for the Continental Gin Company at ten cents per hour.

While on the farm I attended community singing schools. In 1902 I attended a Normal Singing School taught by Prof. J. Henry Showalter, and a year later was secretary of another taught by him. I attended Mississippi College during the session of 1905-06. The next year I went to Moody Bible Institute to study music, but was unable to finish the course on account of my eyes. In 1911 I studied voice with George J. Parker of Boston and later with Dr. Andrew Hemphill of Fort Worth. I received the Mus.B. degree in 1918 from the Siegel-Myers University Correspondence School of Music. The degree of Mus.D. was conferred on me by the Southern School of Fine Arts in 1942.

My conversion was in a children's meeting in a Cumberland Presbyterian Church in my home community in Alabama, and six years later when my parents were converted I joined that church with them. In 1904 my wife and I joined the North Highlands Baptist Church in Birmingham and were baptized by Rev. Hatcher Watkins. I was a charter member of the Seminary Hill Baptist Church and served as chairman of its board of deacons.

Work as an evangelistic singer began with Rev. Otto Barber in 1904, and the next year I was employed in that capacity by the Mississippi Baptist State Mission Board. In 1906 I was associated with Rev. E. D. Solomon in revival work. Later I did evangelistic singing under Dr. E. B. Towner, Director of Music at Moody Bible Institute. In the winter of 1909 I was sent to the Panama Canal Zone in a similiar capacity by the Southern Baptist Home Mission Board. On returning in the spring I was put on the staff of the Home Mission Board as evangelistic singer with Dr. Weston Bruner, Superintendent of Evangelism.

I have directed choirs in several churches including the Twenty-seventh Street Baptist Church in Birmingham, the First Baptist Church, Wesson, Mississippi, and Seminary Hill and Broadway Baptist Churches in Fort Worth. Also I have directed the Seminary Choral Club in presenting at Christmas, commencement and other occasions *The Messiah* forty times, *The Elijah* and *Ruth* ten times each, and *The Creation, Holy City, King of Kings, Seven Last Words of Christ* and other outstanding selections from time to time.

My first marriage was in 1900 to Miss Velma Burns of Alabama who died along with our infant daughter in 1906. While attending the Southern Baptist Convention at Oklahoma City in May, 1912, I met Miss Lura Mae Hawk, a member of the choir of the First Baptist Church there, and we were married the following July. To this union was born a daughter, Lurames, now the wife of Lieut. Le Moyne Michels. They have two fine children.

In 1915 President L. R. Scarborough asked me to become head of the Department of Gospel Music of the Southwestern Baptist Theological Seminary. The work grew, other teachers were added, and curricula outlined leading to the Diploma and Bachelor's and Master's degrees in Sacred Music. In 1921 the department became a school and in 1926 George E. Cowden Hall was erected to house it. The faculty began with two and grew to be fifteen. The student body started with nine and has grown to two hundred. The school is a member of the Texas State Music Association and eligible for membership in the National Association of Schools of Music. It has enrolled more than 2,500 students during the years, and graduated over 250,

who are now located in churches, schools, and on mission fields
From time to time I have held membership in a number of
organizations of various kinds, including denominational groups,
the Kiwanis Club, The Order of the Eastern Star, Knight
Templars in the Masonic Order, Fort Worth Music Teachers'
Association, (past president), Texas State Music Teachers'
Association, Tri-State Church Music Association, National Music Education Conference, Authors' and Composers' Association of America and several others, local and general. I have
served on the Southern Baptist Church Music Committee and
spoken at Southern music conferences at Ridgecrest and
the National Music Convention in Los Angeles. My name is
in the *Encyclopedia of Musicians* and *Who's Who in America.*

Besides five mimeographed books used in class work at the
Seminary I have published *Practical Church Music* (1925),
Ministry of Music (1928), *Church Music* (1935), *Music and
the Scriptures* (1942), and the *Choir in the Now Liturgical
Church,* and served as an editor of *Jehovah's Praise, and Kingdom Songs.* Also I have written two sacred music dramas,
four sacred music cantatas, and many anthems, hymns, and gospel songs, and articles on music for various denominational
papers.

In the summer of 1945 I completed thirty years with Southwestern Baptist Theological Seminary, and retired as Director
of the School of Sacred Music on account of health. I am now
living at 801 Page St., Fort Worth, Texas, and giving my time
as strength permits to writing, teaching in music training schools
and lecturing in church music conferences.

CHURCH MUSIC TENDENCIES OF TODAY*

From the dawn of creation, when the morning stars sang together (Job 38:7), music has been a vital factor in religious worship. The kind of music used has depended very largely, if not entirely, upon the extent of the cultural development of the people by whom it was used. Without music, Christian worship and service would be bereft of one of their most helpful and powerful agencies in spreading the gospel of Christ. The music used in the Christian religion differs from that used in all other religions in that it is a means of praise, adoration, and exaltation of the King of Kings.

Andrew Law says, "Theology and music move hand in hand into time, and will continue eternally to illustrate, embellish, enforce, impress, and fix in the mind of the grand and great truths of Christianity." It seems to be part of the divine plan that music should be the handmaid of the churches. The Reverend David R. Breed, in his book on hymnology, *The History and Use of Hymns and Hymn Tunes,* says, "The fundamental difficulty is that we do not realize how much sacred song is to us, what it means, what it expresses, and what it is capable of accomplishing; and, therefore, it is pitiably neglected."

During the early centuries of Christianity, music was a powerful aid in carrying on the work of the churches. Under stress of bitter persecution some of the greatest hymns were given birth. It is said that the barbarians were won and transformed by the singing of Christian hymns. Edwards says, "It was the Hymns of Ambrose that conquered Constantine."

The Reformation directed by Luther was accomplished largely through the singing of Luther's hymns. Cardinal Cajetan said of him, "By his songs he has conquered us." and, in connection with the founding of Methodism by the Wesleys, it is said that when blood-thirsty crowds could not be quelled by John Wesley's black eyes or by Whitfield's compelling voice, they were known to turn and slink away when the truth was sung to them in Charles Wesley's hymns. Their leaders were known to weep and groan with remorse under the influence of Wesley's singing. They took the preacher by the hand and

*Article in *Music Journal*, November, 1945.

went away arm in arm, swearing by all that was good that not a hair of his head should be touched.

In the present age, no one would attempt to deny the power and influence of music in all Christian activity. An effective music program puts the worshipper in a receptive mood for the truths which the minister presents in his sermons. It also works on the emotions and affects the will in such a way that the individual is responsive to the teachings of Christ.

A very conservative estimate of the time consumed by the music program in each period of the church service—Sunday school, young people's meetings, evangelistic meetings, and all other activities—is about one-third of the whole time.

An impressive number of people are directly or indirectly connected with the music program as church music directors, choir directors, choir members, song leaders, accompanists, and leaders and performers on orchestral instruments. For instance, my own denomination, Southern Baptists, has over 25,000 churches and a membership of some 6,000,000 persons. Each of these churches has a choir director or song leader; each of them has an accompanist. Allowing an average of ten choir members for each of the 25,000 churches, there would be approximately 250,000 choir members, making a grand total of 300,000 people who are directly connected with the music program of the churches in the Southern Baptist Convention.

An imporant factor to be considered is the financial outlay for the music programs in the churches. Professor Augustine Smith, of Boston University, says that in the churches of America there is an annual outlay of $30,000,000 on religious music and that, because of the lack of standards, 90 percent of the amount is wasted. As applied to the Southern Baptist churches, the author believes that a conservative estimate of the cost of music programs, including hymnals, songbooks, choral music, cantatas, oratorios, instrumental music, instruments of various kinds, and the salaries of choir direrctors, song leaders, orchestra and band leaders, accompanists, soloists, quartets, and choirs would be $1,000,000 annually, or an average of $40 for each church. And if Professor Smith's statement that 90 per cent is lost because of inadequate and in-effective music programs is correct, then Southern Baptists are responsibile for wasting $900,000 a year.

Much has been said and written regarding the forms of music used in nonliturgical church programs, and much more could and should be said and written about them. The early Christians used the Psalms with tunes handed down from the Hebrew worship.

In the second century A. D. they began to compose their own songs, which expressed a distinctly Christian sentiment. In the fourth century the Roman Church, declared by the Roman emperor to be the Church of State, established all over its domain church music schools in which singers were trained to take charge of the music programs of the church. According to the records, for about one thousand years music was fostered entirely by the Roman church fathers.

In the sixteenth century Martin Luther broke away from the established forms and gave congregational singing to the people in their native tongue. Dr. Louis Benson, in his book *The English Hymn: Its Development and Use,* says that some other sects prior to the Reformation sang congregational songs in their own tongue. Luther wrote hymns based upon scriptural texts and set to tunes composed by himself, or to some of the German choral tunes. Other Protestant groups used the Psalms, unaltered, set to music. It was during the reign of Henry VIII that the Church of England came into existence, and it followed the forms of the Roman church to a great extent.

Isaac Watts appeared upon the scene the latter part of the seventeenth century with arrangements of the Psalms in metrical forms and hymns written on scriptural texts. Charles Wesley joined Watts in the early part of the eighteenth century, and together they brought in the era of English hymnody which earned them the title the Fathers of English Hymnody. The masses took to the hymn form, but the conservatives tried to stem the tide. Watts and Wesley were followed by hosts of other hymn writers. Hymn singing became universal in Protestant churches. Psalm singers were the last to adopt the hymns. The introduction of hymn singing and instruments in the churches brought about a great change in worship music. In the early part of the nineteenth century the gospel song was introduced in America.

At the present time the nonliturgical churches are widely divided in their likes, dislikes, and uses of church music. There are two distinct types, almost as far apart as the North and South Poles. The large urban churches with wealthy memberships desire a very formal type of service and a music program presented by the best trained choirs. The churches in smaller communities, with congregations made up of people who have had little opportunity to gain a knowledge and appreciation of music, prefer a simple type of music, often with little more than doggerel for words and with an ultra-rhythmical melody which appeals more to the physical than to the spiritual. In between these extremes is the great group of average churches, most of which eventually find themselves in one or the other of the extreme groups.

It is a sad fact that most of our churches become a prey to the commercial songbook publishers which usually means that they succumb to a poor grade of church music. In many of these there is opposition to the anthem on the grounds that it is not spiritual although the real truth is that most anthems are scriptural in nature, scriptures set to music. It is heartening indeed to note, however, that there is a definite trend in most of our churches, especially from the average church to the "First Churches," toward a better church music program, one that is more worshipful and less rhythmical, the norm being the standard hymn with opportunity for anthems and Gospel songs.

There is a growing demand in churches for music leadership trained in the Westminster Choir School, Christiansen Choir School, and similar superior choir schools. Another indication of the upward trend in church music throughout the country is that so many schools (the writer has noted twenty-three) are offering courses in church music and many of them offer church music degrees. The church leadership—preachers, education workers, and musicians—of the future must be able to promote and maintain programs commensurate with the ideals, standards, and appreciation of the young people of today. This applies to rural as well as urban communities.

SECURING BETTER MUSIC IN WORSHIP*

This is one of the most vital questions facing the churches of today, especially the non-liturgical churches. However, it is one of the most difficult to discuss because of its many angles and the differences of opinion on the subject. Too, it is a result that cannot be obtained overnight; to be lasting it must come by way of a gradual educational process. The speaker can bring only a few suggestions which are the result of study, observation and personal experience.

The first general suggestion relates to the matter of training and guiding our people into the knowledge of the purpose and mission of church music. That God gave it to be used as one medium through which to express our religious emotions—praise, adoration, joy, thanksgiving, devotion—must be impressed upon them. The mission of church music is the same as the mission of the church: to bring others into a fuller knowledge of Christ as Saviour, Master and Lord.

Also, the people should be taught to love and appreciate the better types of hymns. An appreciation of a thing is the greatest incentive to use it, and appreciation comes through education, influence and atmosphere or surroundings that are conducive to it. So we should teach good hymns to all age groups in our church life.

The churches, also, should have in them a church music educational program paralleling the secular music educational program just as they now have a religious educational program. By this means children and young people will be trained into an understanding of the best music. This will aid greatly in growing an appreciation for the better hymns. Results for helpfulness will follow.

Physical equipment should include an instrument—organ or piano in good repair and well tuned—, an adequate lighting system by which the singers can easily read music, and an abundant supply of worthy hymn books. The last-mentioned is important. Before we can have better hymn-singing we must have better hymnals from which to sing. Too many of our

*Address delivered at National Educators' Music Conference, Los Angeles, 1940.

non-liturgical churches, as in the case of our own denomination, are a prey to the cheap song book publishers.

The minister, his official board, and the church have much to do with inducing the use of better hymns in the church service. Unless there is a strong, sympathetic support of this movement little can be accomplished. In fact, the speaker believes the crux of the matter lies here. If the preacher has been the pastor of a church for sometime, the music conditions prevailing in the various departments of the church life are but reflections of his appreciation and desires.

Much depends upon the efficiency and ability of the music director and accompanist in securing the use of better hymns in the church service and related activities. In order to be a good salesman of any make of automobile, the salesman must first be sold on that particular car himself. Before the music leader will be able to get people to sing and enjoy and use better hymns he must be "sold" on them himself—have a love and appreciation for them.

The director, or song leader, must have had preparation for the work in his field—spiritually and mentally—with a physically fit body. Some of the essential qualifications are: magnetism, creative imagination, cheerfulness, a sense of humor, initiative and an earnest desire to leave off those personal habits which hinder his work.

Without a good accompanist it is practically impossible to carry on a successful music program. Church music playing is an art within itself and must be studied if perfected. The same religious and educational qualifications as those required for the director are desirable for the accompanist. Too, he or she must have a keen sense of measure and rhythm, be able to build a good accompaniment from the harmonies arranged for the voice parts, not drown out the voices, not sacrifice the spiritual for the artistic (but make the work more spiritual through artistic methods), be subordinate to the director, be able to memorize readily, make the best of the instrument at hand, and be on time and regular in attendance.

Following are some suggested methods which may be employed as an incentive to use better hymns in our church services:

1. Selection of hymns which produce an emotional reaction, instead of a physical reaction.

2. Selection of hymns appropriate for the occasion.

3. Teaching the congregation that in hymns the sentiment of the text is paramount, the music an aid in conveying the thought of the text, and the text and music properly suited to each other.

4. There should be variety in the rendering and use of hymns. This may be obtained by solos, duets, trios, quartets, women's voices, men's voices, children's voices, unison and antiphonal singing, humming back of solo voice, reading words while instrument plays, song sermons arranged homiletically around a given theme, or a song service built around a subject, and hymn-author studies with a brief biographical sketch before the hymn is sung.

5. Regardless of what method is employed the dignity of the occasion should be preserved. Uncouthness or vaudeville performance should never be reverted to in the singing of great religious hymns. Cheapness never aids the religious spirit on any occasion in any service. Stamping the foot, slapping the hands or the song book, yelling "sing it", whistling, or wearing a forced smile, attract the attention to the leader rather than what he is trying to do.

Let us "praise Jehovah in the beauty of holiness. . . Praise ye the Lord!"

CHAPTER XI

L. R. SCARBOROUGH

BIOGRAPHICAL SKETCH*

The Baptist world has a new reason for celebrating the Fourth of July, since on that day in 1870, in a humble home in Colfax, Louisana, Lee Rutland Scarborough was born. The parents were. Mr. George W. and Mrs. Rutland Scarborough. He was a born leader of men. It made no difference with what group he associated, he became their leader.

His life may be. divided into three periods. The first is that of preparation. An all-wise Father provided this preparation. God guided the Scarborough family to the big, open west near Anson, Texas, where they settled. Here, young Lee. Rutland got the training that was indispensable to his future greatness. He lived in a dug-out. His early life was that of a typical cowboy. He. was active in annual "round-ups", was a frequenter of the chuck wagon, followed cattle herds, and learned all the things incident to cowboy life, including "cutting out cows and calves", and "branding and marking".

In that period it was the "wild and woolly" west. Here the young lad learned to hunt wild game, turkey, deer, anthlope, and bear, and to ride. Someone has said, "He could ride anything that wore hair, whether cattle or horses". This outdoor life gave him a strong and healthy body. Few men could stand up under harder strain. God knew that a strong body would be needed when the young man became a national leader.

The young lad received such schooling as was common in that locality. He then went to Baylor University, receiving the B. A. degree in 1892. In 1896 he received the B. A. degree from Yale University, and went to Cameron, Texas, as pastor. Then he attended Southern Seminary one year. His mind had

*By Rev. Perry F. Evans, Field Representative Buckner Orphan's Home.

been set on becoming a great lawyer but God intervened. "You are a chosen vessel of mine to preach the unsearchable riches of Christ."

Perhaps his little semi-invalid mother did more to influence him religiously than any other person. But when he met and married Miss Neppie Warren, she, perhaps, had the greatest influence over him. "Behind the success of every man is a little woman, somewhere." Mrs. L. R. Scarborough is a most patient and Godly woman. She has never sought the limelight nor the spectacular. She has been content to live through her famous husband and six lovely children.

The second period is that of evangelism. In this realm Dr. Scarborough was perhaps greatest. He had few equals in the nation. His passion for the lost was supreme and challenging to the last degree. It was akin to Paul who said, "Brethren, my heart's desire and prayer to God for Israel is that they might be saved . . . I could wish myself accursed from Christ for my brethren in the flesh." Outside of Dr. George W. Truett, the writer of this article has never met another who had such an unutterable yearning for the lost. While in the pastorate he not only kept his church seeking them, but assisted scores of other Baptist pastors in revivals. He held some of the really great revivals of the nation.

His evangelistic efforts headed up in a constructive program. His revivals aided churches, hospitals, seminaries, and other agencies. He took into his warm heart all agencies. As president of Southwestern Seminary he continued to hold "The Chair of Fire," and from the classroom of evangelism went out men and women around the world fired with a passion to win the lost.

The third period of his life is that of kingdom building. Dr. Scarborough had no superior and few equals in all the South in this respect. While he was pastor of the great First Church, Abilene, he found time to raise money for two buildings for Simmons University. All of the buildings on the Southwestern campus are the results of his labors. Every brick in their walls is bathed with blood, sweat and tears.

Without doubt his greatest achievement in Kingdom building was his leadership in the Seventy-Five Million Campaign.

One day he told the writer: "Perry, my brethren tell me I must move my headquarters to Nashville, Tennessee." There he began the Herculean task of setting up an organization. In an almost unbelievably short time he swung into battle line the Baptists of the South, Marshalling his forces, including Baptist papers, the State Conventions, Training Unions, Sunday Schools and W.M.U.'s not only did he reach his goal but went far beyond securing gifts and pledges of ninety-two million dollars.

Some of his chief characteristics were his passion for the lost; already discussed; his optimism—Pollyana herself could have taken lessons from him: his keen sense of humor; even under the most trying circumstances; and his approachableness, being as much so as a little child.

Dr. Scarborough received the D.D. from Baylor and the LL.D. from Union University. He was president of the Texas Baptist Convention, and the Southern Baptist Convention, and vice-president of the Baptist World Alliance. He was author of *Recruits for World Conquests, With Christ after the Lost, Marvels of Divine Leadership, The Tears of Jesus, Prepare to Meet Thy God, Endued to Win, Christ's Militant Kingdom, Holy Places and Precious Promises, How Jesus Won Men, Ten Spiritual Ships, Products of Pentecost, My Conception of the Gospel Ministry. A Blaze of Evangelism across the Equator,* and *A Modern School of the Prophets.* He died at Amarillo, Texas, April 10, 1945, and was buried at Fort Worth.

THE TEARS OF JESUS*

John 11:35 — Jesus Weeping at the Gate of Death. "Jesus Wept."

Luke 19:41 — Jesus Weeping over a Doomed City. "When he was come near, he beheld the city, and wept over it."

Heb. 5:7 — Jesus Weeping over a Lost World. "He offered up prayers and supplication with strong crying and tears unto him that was able to save him from death, and was heard in that he feared."

We find in this first scripture Jesus weeping at the grave of Lazarus. In the second scripture we see Him weeping over a city which being doomed had rejected His message. And in the last scripture we find Him shedding tears and offering prayers in the days of His flesh over a ruined world for which He was to die.

We note in this second scripture that he was coming to Jerusalem for the last time. He had been out among the people for three and a half years, preaching, teaching, healing and performing many miracles. The blind could see when he touched their eyes; the lame could walk, the dumb could speak, and the dead came forth out of the grave at His word of authority and power. But He had come now to Jerusalem, for the last time. Just a few days afterwards he was to be crucified in the city he had come to save. Coming in that morning from the east side, with a great crowd meeting and following Him, praising God in accordance with the promises concerning Him, He saw that beautiful city with a wonderful history.

I am sure, since He knew all things, there was present in His mind the past history of triumphs and defeat, of prosperity and adversity. I am sure that He saw with His historic mind the things that had transpired in that city, where a great people had builded a great city, the center of the religious life of the world, where He had trained a race to be His chosen people. And as He looked upon that city the Scriptures say, "He wept." This Son of God, this Son of Man, seeing that city wept bitter, briny tears over what He saw. This is one of the three times

*From *The Tears of Jesus* by L. R. Scarborough, Baptist Sunday School Board. Used by permission.

in the Scriptures where it speaks of the tears of Jesus. On one occasion before this he stood at the grave of Lazarus, and wept, joined in the sorrow of the loved ones for the man who had been hospitable to Him, a man He loved. And there the Son of Man at the gate of death shed tears.

The other place where it speaks of His tears is where I read you from the 5th chapter of Hebrews. It says that "in the days of His flesh with strong supplication and tears he prayed unto Him Who was able to save Him from death." There in that case Jesus Christ not only wept over a lost city, but He wept over a lost world.

Now I want us to think for a little while of the weeping Saviour, the tears of Jesus Christ.

I. Why Are These Tears?

Who is this strange person who has filled all history and yet standing on the crest of the mountain we see weeping? His heart is torn and there comes from His eyes and from His heart tears that represent the attitude of His soul toward a lost city and toward a lost world. Who is He? Why He is the author of our Bible, the founder of our churches, a refuge to our souls, the hope of our resurrection, the builder of our heaven, and the source and provider of all our spiritual blessings. The Scriptures call Him our advocate, the anointed one, the balm in Gilead for our souls, the bread of life for our hopes, the corner stone and the foundation of our lives, the commander of God's army which is to conquer all sin, the counsellor and guide for our feet.

He is the founder on which we build and the fountain from which we drink. He is the hiding place for our tempest-tossed souls, the high priest of our communion with God. He is the Immanuel, the very presence of the Most High. He is King over Kings and Lord over Lords. He was the Lamb of God slain from before the foundation of the world as a sacrifice and atonement for our sins. He is the leader of God's mightiest hosts, the Lion of the Tribe of Judah. He it was that was the Man of Sorrows and who was aquainted with grief. He is the conquerer over sin and the enemies of God, the mediator between man and God, the messenger of God's covenant to a

lost world, the Messiah of hope for a coming day of full redemption. He is the Prince of Life and the Prince of Peace,
the redeemer, the rock of ages, the rose of Sharon, the scepter
of Israel, the shepherd of God's sheep. He is God's only begotten and most beloved son.

Here on the mount overlooking Jerusalem He weeps with a
heart full of compassion and love for a lost world, and estab-
lishes again the doctrine of the chief and central passion of
the gospel wrought out in His ministry, death and intercession
for a sin-cursed world. He is the mightiest among the mighty
and loveliest among ten thousand, the maker and preserver of
our lives and the Saviour of our souls. He it is that weeps over
our sin, doom and destiny. It is in His hands that the reins of
the universe are held. This man is the Son of God, is very
God himself. He it is who controls all the things of our lives.
And yet yonder in the city where He had taught and preached
and was soon to be crucified, we see Him shedding the bitterest
of tears. He is not some conqueror come to destroy, but a
Saviour come to save. He will not call down the wrath of the
clouds and gather the powers of the storms over them and die
for them and save them. He it is that is weeping today over a
lost world.

I raise another question.

II. Why These Tears?

Why is that this Son of Man, this Son of God, is weeping
over the city of Jerusalem, and was constantly during the days
of His flesh appealing unto God with strong supplications and
tears? I say to you He is not weeping for Himself, though He
sees the shadow of the cross just ahead of Him. He sees the
dark, unspeakable sorrow of Gethsemane through which He is
to go, the cruel crown of thorns which is to be pressed on His
head, and already the piercing of the nails in His hands and the
sword in His side. Yet He is not weeping over Himself. He
is not weeping like a defeated conqueror. He was not weeping
over a life of defeat, though in the eyes of the world He was
living a life of defeat. He was not weeping because of His own
failure or because of any discontent in His heart. Jesus was
not weeping for Himself; but He was weeping because He saw

some things from the Mount of Olivet. He was not weeping over that city which through the centuries had been builded by the sacrifices, and labors of His people. He was not weeping for its reputation, though He saw the ruin of that city about which He here prophesied. He was not weeping for the falling walls and the ruins of the Temple. Why was He weeping that day? What was it that He saw that caused the tears to come from His eyes? It is about that that I wish to speak to you.

I want if I can to bring you this day into a sympathetic attitude with Jesus Christ, as He stood on Mount Olive. What was it that brought the tears from His eyes and broke His heart? It lies in three directions. In the first place, he wept because He saw the spiritual condition of men. He saw men in their sins. He saw them in the darkness of their unbelief, in the night of their unfaith in Him, sinners, dead in trespasses and sins. He saw the wrath of God on them if the love of God was not in their hearts. He saw them rejecting the only light come to them. He saw them without hope and without God in the world. As He looked upon the soul of an unbeliever no wonder it brought a desire to be crucified for the life and salvation of that individual. The condition of men today ought to bring tears and burdens to the hearts of God's people.

I stood the other day by the side of a wife as she looked upon the pale, emaciated face of her loving husband. The doctors had just operated on him and said he had typhoid fever. At that time he was suffering from a hemorrhage which it looked like he could not stand. His face was white and his finger tips and toe tips seemed to be drained of blood. I stood by her side as we went into another room to pray. Oh, there was such a wringing of the wife's heart as she said, "He cannot stand the loss of blood! He cannot stand the battle of the germs of disease in his body!" She realized the condition of her husband.

I stood by the side of a mother as she looked into the face of her baby, dying as she thought. Her heart was wrung. The doctors had said, "He must die." She was torn by the realization of the condition of her child.

I will tell you, my friends, we need today to look into

the lives of the unsaved men all about us and see their peril
and condition before Almighty God. Every man, woman and
young person in this community without Jesus Christ in his
heart by faith, is lost and dead in trespasses and in sins, is away
from God and has no hope. The immoral decay of sin, is in
every particle of his spirit. Shall we look on them unmoved
while the Son of God seeing a lost and ruined city shed tears
over its condition? I trust that God's people seeing the unsaved about them today and during this meeting will join the
Saviour weeping over a lost world.

I shall never forget one Sunday afternoon, (after I had
preached in the morning), when my first child, just five years
of age, a little boy, as I was lying on my bed was sitting astride
my body. Suddenly he changed the subject from what we
had been talking about and looking into my face said with a
trembling voice, "Daddy, I am lost. I want you to show me
the way to Christ." I do not explain it. I only tell you the
story. It was the first time I realized the spiritual condition of
my child. It was the first time he had appealed to me from his
own lost soul. From that time until he was saved I kept the
prayers hot up, up to God. I carried him to the Saviour day
by day. I believe it was because of the concern created in
my heart that day that I kept the prayers hot. I want us in
these days to remember the spiritual condition of every man
that does not know Jesus Christ.

I think another thing that stirred the heart of Jesus was
not only the condition of men, but the destiny of men. He saw
the place to which these people were going when they were
carried to the cemeteries. He the Son of God was thinking of
where those people were going after death. And it is a matter
that should stir our hearts. It is not what we possess here,
not how much education or how little we have, but the question
of destiny, of where we are going. This should be the important question. It matters not that we die. How little value
there is to the bodies of men, how little value!

But my friends it is the eternal destiny of the soul that is the
important question. I want us to know in the battle that we
are going to fight here within the next few days that we are
fighting a battle for the destinies of men. Every unsaved man

in your community is going to hell. I do not know how you
feel. I bless God I know there is a heaven for those who believe in Christ. I am going to preach the gospel on this point.
I want us to see the destinies of men and be moved like our
Saviour was moved.

There was another thing that stirred the heart of our Saviour
and that was their refusal to hear Him and their rejection of
Him. Oh, the saddest thing that can come to the heart of
Jesus Christ is for Him to be rejected! I wonder what will be
the attitude of the people of the community. He had wrought
among them and yet they had rejected Him. I tell you, there
is a demonstration on every hand that Jesus Christ is the Son
of God and the Saviour of the world. I wonder what we will
do with this demonstration the next few days.

This incident in the life of the Saviour but illustrates the
care Jesus has for men.

III. The Savior's Care.

He has shown, not only in His earthly life and sacrificial
death, but in His heavenly ministry for these twenty centuries
how much He cares for men. Even the hairs of our heads are
numbered and not a sparrow falls without His loving care.
Every detail of our lives is of interest to the Saviour and all
those things that make for our salvation and spiritual strength
and service for Him are of the deepest concern to our Saviour's
heart.

Does He not show in His attitude at Lazarus' grave that
He loves and cares for the suffering loved ones at every grave?
Does He not show by the many examples of healing, of raising
the dead, of straightening the limbs of the crippled, opening
the eyes of the blind and the ears of the deaf, that He cares for
our bodies and our souls? Never a tear falls from the heart of
a sorrowing widow nor from the penitent soul of the sick sinner
that misses the loving eye of our Saviour. He has assured us
by His multiplied providences of loving care. That is the beauty
of that great picture on Mount Olivet. Jesus loves men and
has a concern for their salvation. He has shown it in His
creative power, in His preserving and providential power, in
His earthly ministry and in His death on Calvary.

You and I should take up the work of Jesus Christ and

care for lost men. This is the message that I bring you this morning. This is the message—do you care for the lost men and women of this city? I wonder how many of you do. Will you stand with Jesus on Mount Olivet today and say, "We, too, will weep for our loved ones and join our Saviour in caring for their souls?"

Some time ago I was in a great convention. I spoke to that convention on compassion for the lost. It was some years ago when our boys were gathering in the army camps all over our country. In that crowd was a rather old, plainly dressed woman. She and her husband came down the aisle to shake hands with me. She took me by the hand and said, "Do you live at Fort Worth?" I said, "I do." Then she started to say, "My boy is in Camp Bowie near Fort Worth." She stopped and wept.

Seeing her weeping her husband came up and putting his arm around her, he said, "Mary, what's the matter?" She said, "I was thinking of our baby boy yonder in Camp Bowie. You know he isn't saved. We have written letters to him about it. We have prayed for him and others have prayed for him." She said "Here's a preacher that lives near where our soldier boy is and I was trying to put our boy, our baby boy, on the heart of this preacher." Then she turned to me in a way and with a question I shall never forget. I thought I loved lost men. For twenty-five years I have given strength without reservation to the winning of lost men to Christ. I thought I loved lost men. But this dear old mother looked up with all the love of a mother and said, "Preacher, do you love lost men?" Oh, that question rings in my heart today!

You have made great preparation for this meeting and I bless God for it. The great question now is, Do we love lost men? If we do, God help us to join Jesus Christ in soul-agony for them that we may win them to Him. I wonder how many of you can say: "Deep down in my heart I do have a tender, affectionate concern for the unsaved of this community and I can join with my Savior in a deep compassion for their salvation."

Listen to what God says, "They that sow in tears shall reap in joy. He that goeth forth and weepeth, bearing precious seed, shall doubtless come again with rejoicing, bringing his sheaves with him." God help us to be stirred in our souls for the lost of this community.

CHAPTER XII

C. B. WILLIAMS

AUTOBIOGRAPHICAL SKETCH

I was born in Cambden County, N. C., January 15, 1869. My father, Simeon Walston Williams, was distantly related to Roger Williams, father of religious liberty in America; William Williams, signer of the Declaration of Independence; Sir George Williams, founder of the Young Men's Christian Association; and William Williams, author of "Guide Me, O Thou Great Jehovah."

My mother, Mary Bray Williams, was descended from Prof. Thomas Bray of Cambridge University; Robert Bray, a naval officer whose ship (Columbia) carried the first American flag around the world; and William Bray, a charter member of Old Shiloh Church, the oldest Baptist Church in North Carolina, organized in 1727.

I taught in a country school when fifteen years of age at $20.00 per month and paid off the mortgage on the old family homestead. At eighteen I entered Wake Forest College with $48.00, borrowed $150.00 from the local educational board, and graduated with a debt of only $150.00. While in college I was active in debating and literary society work, and was valedictorian of the class of 1891. My four-year average scholastic record was $98\frac{1}{2}$ which was not surpassed for forty years.

I was licensed to preach when seventeen years of age, and held several country church revivals that year. Three years later I was ordained by the Wake Forest Baptist Church, having been called as pastor of the church at Brasfield. For five years following graduation I was pastor of the Winton Baptist Church, principal of the school, and raised the money for a new school building.

In 1897 I entered Crozer Theological Seminary, specialized in the original languages of the Bible, and graduated in 1900 with the B.D. degree, my thesis being on "Evolution and God". Among the teachers there were Henry G. Weston, Bayard Taylor and Milton G. Evans. While there I was pastor of Baptist churches in Chester, Pa., and in nearby New Jersey cities.

Soon after graduating from Crozer I started for Texas, but stopped over in Locksburg, Arkansas, and served as principal of the high school for a year. After another year as pastor of the Olive Street Baptist Church in Texarkana, I was called to the pastorate of the First Baptist Church of Stephenville, Texas, and served for three years, when I accepted the pastorate at Rockdale. During this time I held revivals in Dublin, Lampasas, Brownwood and Trinity resulting in over 300 professions.

In 1905 Dr. B. H. Carroll, then Dean of the Theological School of Baylor University, wired me to meet him in Waco for an interview. I did, and before the day of consultation was over was elected to the chair of Greek New Testament and Interpretation and began work enthusiastically the following week. I was thus the first one brought in from the outside for Southwestern Seminary, Dr. B. H. Carroll and Dr. A. H. Newman being already connected with Baylor University. Others were soon added to the staff.

While teaching at Baylor I attended summer schools in the University of Chicago receiving the M.A. degree in 1907 and the Ph.D. in 1908. In 1916 I delivered the Baccalaureate address at Baylor and received the D.D. degree. In 1920 the trustees there voted to confer the LL.D., but being in a financial campaign as president of Howard College I was unable to be present to receive it.

While at Baylor the First Baptist Church of Waco offered me the pastorate at a salary of $4,000, but I declined and stayed with teaching at a $1,500 salary. After moving to Fort Worth I was called to the Broadway Baptist Church there and the First Baptist Church in Wichita Falls at salaries three times that of the Seminary salary. In nine years in Fort Worth I raised $75,000 for seminary expenses and endowment and witnessed in one service at the military camp 200 professions.

I was made the first librarian at Southwestern and catalogued the first 5,000 volumes of its excellent library, given by

Drs. A. J. Harris and A. H. Newman. From 1913 to 1919 I
served as dean of the Seminary, and managing editor of the
"Southwestern Journal of Theology" in addition to my teaching. Also I served during summers as dean of the Panhandle
Bible Conference.

In 1919 I resigned my position at Southwestern to accept
the presidency of Howard College. In two years there I paid
off a debt of $60,000, raised an additional $300,000 for endowment, and got the college accredited by the Southern Association. I resigned the presidency of Howard in 1921 to return
to teaching, research and writing.

I served as professor at Mercer University from 1921 to
1925 and at Union University from 1925 to 1938, when I retired from teaching. Then I served as pastor in Florida and
North Carolina for seven years. I am now making my home
at Pierson, Florida, and writing *An Estimate of the Greatness
of Dr. B. H. Carroll.*

The books I have written are *A History of Baptists in North
Carolina, The Function of Teaching in Christianity, New Testament History and Literature, Citizens of Two Worlds, An Introduction to New Testament Literature, The Evolution of New
Testament Christology. A Translation of the New Testament in
the Language of the People, New Testament Synonyms* and
The Galilean Wins.

I have held membership in "The International Society of
Biblical Literature and Exegesis", "The Victorian Institute",
"The Philosophical Society of Great Britain", and others. I am
also listed in *Who's Who in America, Who's Who in American
Education, Who's Who in the American Clergy,* and *Who's
Who Among North America Authors.*

HOW MUCH MORE THEN IS A MAN WORTH!
Matthew 12:12*

The Greek word "man" used here is a generic term. It embraces woman also, and so includes the whole human race. So the sentence would literally read, "How much more then is a human being worth!"

The Greeks, with all their culture and philosophy, had reached no adequate conception of the value of a man, unless he were a Greek. The Romans had no true conception of the real worth of a man, unless he were a Roman. Even the Jews, with a special revelation from God, had failed to reach an adequate conception of the value of a human being, unless he were a Jew.

Jesus, however, taught in universal terms that a human being, of whatever race, condition or character, is of supreme value. Jesus restored the paralyzed arm of a man on the Sabbath, which violated the Pharisaic law. So the Pharisee asked, "Is it lawful to heal on the Sabbath day?" Jesus reminded them that they would lift a sheep out of the pit on the Sabbath to keep if from dying and added "How much more then is a man worth!"

I. Some Human Estimates of the Worth of a Man

We start with the scientific man's estimate—the lowest estimate we know. Alfred Russell Wallace, who, simultaneously with Charles Darwin, gave to the world the theory of evolution, taught that a human being derived his soul directly from God by special creation, but that his body is the product of an evolutionary process. Charles Darwin, an extremist in evolution, still believed that the human being is a creature of God but through the evolutionary process. Thomas Huxley, though an agnostic, claims in his book, *Man's Position in Nature,* man as the climax of all life on earth. Even Ernest Haeckel, a radical German materialistic scientist, who kept a

*A sermon preached at various high school and college commencements and New Orleans Baptist Seminary.

life-size portrait of a monkey on the wall of his study to remind him of his supposed simian ancestors, still placed man in an exalted rank above the lower animals. Thousands of scientific men believe that God created man.

Next, we ask, what is the philosopher's estimate of man? Socrates, Plato, and Aristotle conceived of man as rational and immortal, and in some sense akin to Deity. Likewise, through the centuries following them most Greek, Roman, German, French, English, and American philosophers, think of man as a rational, immortal being. Borden P. Bowne, in his system of philosophy called Personalism, exalted a human being to the highest pinnacle and regarded man's personality as absolutely immortal and imperishable. Also William James in his Pragmatism taught that man alone of all God's creatures on earth is really worth while and that all the forces of nature and culture should conduce to his welfare.

What is the sociologist's estimate? Sociology is one of the latest children born into the family of sciences. But in the last half century sociologists have impressed on us that even a street waif with no bed but the pavement, no pillow but the rocks, is worth while. Even the deadbeat on the streets ought to be trained and given a place in the world.

What is the author's estimate? What does the literary man say? Robert Burns, in describing the struggles and sufferings of a human being, exclaimed: "A man's a man for a' that, for a' that." Man is made for something other than toil, sufferings and disappointment.

Carlyle said: "Man is the center of nature. That is, nature is not properly understood, with all her rivers and oceans, mountains and volcanoes, flowers and sunsets, without putting man at the very center.

Emerson put his estimate in these graphic words: "Man is an encyclopedia of facts." Man is the total expression of physical, intellectual, moral, and spiritual facts.

Pope in his "Essay on Man" says: "The proper study of mankind is man." Not nature, not philosophy, not even theology, but rather the origin, development, destiny and happiness of man.

Shakespeare exclaims in these matchless words:
"What a piece of work is a man! How noble in reason!
How infinite in faculties! In form and moving how
express and admirable! In action how like an angel!
In apprehension how like a god! The beauty of the world,
the paragon of animals."

II. The Divine Estimate of the Worth of a Man

I now come to emphasize the value God Himself puts upon
His man. Go back to the Garden of Eden, and see what God
did that last creation morning. He made man. He had to
create the universe first, and get everything ready for this
exalted being. By creating man last God would say to us,
"Here is my best, my masterpiece." And I will not stickle if
some keenwitted woman should remind me, "Did He not make
woman last, and not man?" I will not retract my argument
if you make woman God's masterpiece. But since the term
"man" in the text includes woman as well as man, it still holds
true that a human being is God's masterpiece in creation.

Out of what did God create man? The record says that
He took of the clay of the garden and shaped it into the form
of a man, i.e. his physical body. But that is not all of a man.
The record says that God breathed into that body the Divine
breath, and in this way Adam became "a living soul." So man
is made of clay plus the breath of God, a thing not true of any
other animal.

God also said to Adam, "Go and subdue all nature, and be
the master of the world," which is a positive proof that God
considers man the highest creature of all creation on earth.

But God's estimate may also be seen in His providence over
the history of the world. It was Carlyle who said, "God did
make this world, and He does forever govern it; the loud roaring
loom of time, without its French revolutions, and without its
Jewish revelations, weaves the vesture thou sees Him by." We
might add to this marvelous statement that the history of the
world, with its Greek and Roman, American and French, and
German and South American revolutions, and with its Jewish
and Christian revelations, has been directed by the hand of
God for the improvement and happiness of man.

But the sublimest exhibition of God's evaluation of man is the Father's gift of His only begotten Son to die on Calvary, to redeem and save lost men. "For God so loved the world that He gave His only begotten Son, that whosoever believeth on Him might not perish but have eternal life." "When the fullness of time came, God sent forth His Son ... that He might redeem them that were under the law, that we might receive the adoption of sons." Calvary is the most graphic expression of the Father's estimate of man.

What is the Son's estimate? It is His words that are spoken in our text. "How much then is a man of more value than a sheep?" Jesus recognized that man is the greatest animal that came from the creative hand. He is "a living soul." He is made "in the image of God." Then the actions of Jesus speak louder than His words. In life He lifted and comforted, He healed and taught and raised from the dead—all men were the objects of his deeds of mercy.

Horace Mann, the great educator, once delivered a dedicatory address for a million-dollar educational plant. A friend of his said to him, "Horace, like all the orators in your enthusiasm and flights of oratory you say things that are not so." Horace asked, "What did I say today that is not so?" "Oh, you said that if this million-dollar plant should save only one boy it would be money well spent. Bosh! You did not mean such a silly thing as that. The idea of a million-dollar plant saving only one boy and still being a good investment!" Horace pointed his finger in his face and said, "My friend, that depends on whose that boy might be. If it were your boy you would say so." Now Jesus Christ gave, for man's redemption, not millions of dollars, of silver and gold, not jewels and diamonds, but "Himself" to save man.

What is the Holy Spirit's estimate? The Spirit for these thousands of years has been moving up and down the world, from heart to heart, to convince men of sin, teach them the saving truths of the gospel, regenerate the soul, and transform the character and life so as to renew the image of God. How the living actions of the Triune God, the Father, the Son, the Holy Spirit, have demonstrated the lofty estimate of man's incalculable worth!

III. The Sphere of Man's Superior Worth

Wherein lies the superior worth of a man? Is it in his capacity to accumulate wealth? How often do you hear men say, "How much is Mr. Smith worth?" meaning to ask, "How large is his bank account, how many thousands of acres of land has he, how many bonds and stocks?" A man's intrinsic worth cannot be calculated by his capacity to accumulate wealth.

Nor does it lie in the structure of his physical body, though man's physical form is the most symmetrical and most beautiful of all the animals. He "is fearfully and wonderfully made," even from the physical point of view. And yet a lion is much stronger, an elephant is larger, a horse is much fleeter, an eagle can fly more gracefully and swiftly. In the physical realm man is not superior to the lower animals.

Where does his superiority lie? It begins to show itself in his intellect and capacity to think and reason. He can "think God's thoughts after Him." Consider the wonderful thinking of James Watt, who watched the kettle boil and the lid lift, discovered steam, and gave the mighty power to run our trains and ships and other machines; of Franklin, who caught the electric spark from the clouds and gave this mightier power to do man's work; of Morse, who sent the first message over the wires; of Edison, who has made electricity laugh and weep sing and preach; of Marconi, who made electricity encircle the globe without any wires; of Einstein who worked out a mathematical formula so comprehensive as to include the operations of all the laws of the universe; of Arthur Compton and a group of physicists who at last split the atom and produced atomic energy and the atomic bomb.

And what shall I say more! Man's intellectual and research powers seem almost infinite! I stand amazed as I think of what men may accomplish in the next five hundred years, if they continue as they have for the last one hundred. I suspect we shall be able to get into a rocket plane and fly to the moon today and return tomorrow in time to sleep at home. Men have accomplished more than a half dozen scientific miracles—many in the realm of transportation—as marvelous as that.

1. Man's Gift of Speech. He is the only animal on earth that can talk. What a privilege it is to be able to speak—to

put in language our thoughts and feelings! The little lamb can bleat and his mother understands this sheep language; the cow can low and her kind and her master knows her language; the horse can neigh and his fellows and his master recognizes what he means; the dove can coo and the dove family grasps the meaning of the cooing. The parrot approaches human speech, and can imitate, but she cannot express in words her own thoughts (if she has any). Man is the only animal on earth that can think his own thoughts and express them in words, in comprehensible articulate sounds.

A mother whispers words of love to her sobbing child and soothes its shattered nerves and broken heart; a friend speaks words of sympathy to a despairing comrade and lifts his soul to heights of hope. Demosthenes could with his dynamic words of eloquence so inspire the Athenians as to move them to desire to save their country from the ravages of Philip's invading phalanxes. Spurgeon with eloquent words of God's grace moved thousands to conversion to Christ and consecration to God. How much God's program of teaching and evangelizing missions depends upon man's gift of consecrated speech!

2. Man's Capacity for Knowing Right and Wrong. Man has a conscience and is the only being on earth that has such. A mule got mad this morning and kicked his master on the head and left him bleeding and suffering. He is not sorry for it. He has never felt that he did wrong in causing him pain and agony. He has no conscience. Man is the only moral being on earth.

3. Man's Capacity for Worshipping God. This capacity originates in his creation by God in His image. This capacity is universal. Charles Darwin in his voyage around the world reached the conclusion that there was only one or two tribes of savages in Patagonia that did not have some kind of religion. But modern anthropologists have discovered that there is not a single tribe in the jungles of Africa, or in Patagonia, that does not have some form of religion. In other words man is, distinctively, a religious animal. He can pray, he can worship, he can praise his Creator. So far as we know there is not a monkey in the heart of Africa that ever lifted his heart in prayer and praise to his Maker.

4. Man is Immortal. Man is so made as to live on forever. Physical death is not the end of his existence. Regardless of character his existence goes on forever. A human personality can never be destroyed. The pet dog who loves so tenderly, who would die to save his master from the ravages of wild beast, can never rise again to meet his master. That beautiful blooded horse that neighs for his master cannot rise from death to greet him on the other side. The little canary that sings those thrilling notes in the spring time to cheer the heart and make life happier has not a life beyond to sing for you. But you will live right on through death and throughout the ages of eternity.

5. Man is Capable of Eternal Life. This is many steps higher than immortality. All men are immortal. Only those who believe and live in Christ have "eternal life." Man is capable of being "born from above" and having and enjoying eternal life, which is fellowship with God, eternal union and harmony with Him throughout the ceaseless cycles of eternity. This is what the Apostle John means when he exclaims, "Behold, what manner of Love the father hath bestowed upon us, that we should be called children of God, and such we are. Beloved, now are we the children of God, and it is not yet made manifest what we shall be. We know that if He shall be made manifest, we shall be like Him, for we shall see Him as He is." This is eternal life—to be like God, and to see Him as He is through all the ages of eternity.

6. Man's Capacity for Service. In his capacity for eternal life we reached the climax of man's intrinsic worth, but his value of a "servant of all" puts the climax on his worth to the kingdom of God and to his fellowmen. A man, renewed and consecrated, like Paul or Peter or John; like Carey or Judson or Yates; like Spurgeon or Carroll or Truett, is God's most valuable possession, for it is through such as these that He is building His kingdom on earth and saving a world of sinners. The story is told that Gabriel asked Jesus when He ascended to heaven, "How are you going to carry on your work on the earth now?" Jesus replied, "I am depending on Peter, James and John, and the rest of them." "But, suppose they fail you," said Gabriel, then what?" Jesus replied, "I am depending on

them." We are His only dependence.

7. Three Inferences from Man's Superiority. First, he is worth saving phyically and socially. We can produce a stronger race of men by proper birth from proper parentage. If we try we can raise up a superior race of human beings in body and nerves and brains. Jesus looked upon that frail piece of mankind with a withered hand, and was moved with compassion. He must have his limb restored. So He spoke the word and made his withered arm and hand strong.

The church and school must co-operate with medical science and social workers in cleaning up our cities and country that our children may have a wholesome atmosphere in which to live. Our boys and girls must have a good birth and good places to live and play and train for manhood and womanhood.

Secondly, a man is worth saving intellectually and educationally. On John A. Broadus' tomb is this epitaph:
"On earth there is nothing great but man;
In man there is nothing great but mind."
There is nothing on earth that is really great but man, and nothing great in him apart from the soul (including the mind). Then Christian men and women should better support our public schools and colleges, our universities and seminaries, to train and develop the souls of our boys and girls.

Lastly, a man is worth saving spiritually and morally. This is our highest task. Let us build more churches, more Sunday schools. Let us pray that God may call more preachers, more evangelists, more missionaries to carry the gospel around the world, that all the nations and all the races may be brought into the kingdom and lifted to fellowship with God.